Still Starving after all these Years

The Hidden Origins of War, Oppression and Inequality

Still Starving after all these Years

The Hidden Origins of War, Oppression and Inequality

Jeri Studebaker

IFF BOOKS

Winchester, UK
Washington, USA

JOHN HUNT PUBLISHING

First published by iff Books, 2021
iff Books is an imprint of John Hunt Publishing Ltd., No. 3 East Street, Alresford,
Hampshire SO24 9EE, UK
office@jhpbooks.com
www.johnhuntpublishing.com
www.iff-books.com

For distributor details and how to order please visit the 'Ordering' section on our website.

ISBN: 978 1 78904 488 1
978 1 78904 489 8 (ebook)
Library of Congress Control Number: 2019956259

A CIP catalogue record for this book is available from the British Library.

Design: Stuart Davies

UK: Printed and bound by CPI Group (UK) Ltd, Croydon, CR0 4YY
US: Printed and bound by Thomson-Shore, 7300 West Joy Road, Dexter, MI 48130

Contents

In loving memory of my professor and advisor Dr. Erika Bourguignon, who introduced me to indigenous people around the world.

Preface

The purpose of this book is to delve deeply into the mystery of where human groups came from, and how exactly they came to be what they are today. It was written for people who think our species has room for improvement and are hungry for ideas about how to implement the improvement process.

Heartfelt thanks to Dr. Deborah Fleming and Connie Miller for their inspirational comments regarding the manuscript (and many thanks to Connie, too, for the terrific book title).

Introduction

Probably more than any other English-speaking country, America lusts after size. Americans aim for king-sized homes, towering bridges, colossal skyscrapers, bulging bank accounts, and the yawning hollow of the Grand Canyon. Almost anything of size draws us in like bees to honey. On cross-country trips we stop to check out the world's largest ball of string, for example (12 feet in diameter; located in Darwin, Minnesota), the "giant head of Beethoven" in Fort Myers, Florida, the world's largest fishing fly, in Dutch John, Utah, and, in Abilene Texas, the world's largest paper airplane. Clocking in at 135,280 square feet, the Biltmore House in Asheville, North Carolina, beats my little 800-square-foot home by a factor of 170, but Las Vegas' Palazzo Building, with its 6.9-million square-foot interior, dwarfs even the Biltmore.

Americans even have books celebrating size. Among other marvels, *The Guinness Book of World Records* celebrates the world's largest hot dog cart (9 feet, 3 inches by 23 feet, 2 inches, in Union, Missouri), and the world's tallest golf tee (30 feet, 9 inches, Casey, Illinois)(guinnessworldrecords.com).

Americans are big eaters, big shoppers and big collectors. Contests determine who can wolf down the most fruit pies, and stores sponsor "anything you can grab" events with winners allowed to keep all they can pitch into a cart in a ten-minute race around store aisles. And a quick Google search unearths information on the largest collections of Chinese menus, owl-related items, nutcrackers, paper peepshows, and photos of unknown poets.

In other words, it would appear that for Americans "big" is usually better. Except when it isn't.

For every winner in a pie-eating contest, hundreds of thousands fight food-related issues like obesity, bulimia and anorexia. And as many as 25 million Americans are so addicted to shopping that their disorder shreds both their personal finances, and their personal relationships (Benson, 2008: 3–4). What's more, collecting nutcrackers is fine – until you can't stop even after running out of storage space in your home and garage. Unfortunately, millions of Americans find themselves in just such a pickle: with so many things piled so high in their homes, they're forced to squeeze through narrow paths as they inch from one room to another.

This inability to discard possessions, or "hoarding disorder" (HD), afflicts two to six percent of the American population. HD is found not only in America but in other industrialized nations as well, including the UK, Japan, Brazil and Spain (*Mental Health Weekly Digest*, 2018). HD blisters people with a bone-deep urge to save things that usually hold no value for most of us whatsoever, a deep disinclination to discard any of these things, and consequently a problematic home life. Hoarders treasure everything from old newspapers, magazines and mail, to empty boxes, Christmas decorations, and (living) animals. In the past, hoarding disorder was considered part of obsessive-compulsive behavior, but in 2013 the American Psychiatric Association upgraded it to a bona fide mental disorder in its own right (Kress et al., 2016: 83–84).

Another phenomenon related to the strange American relationship with size and quantity: most multi-millionaires consider themselves poor as paupers, believing that financial security will never knock on their door until they amass significantly more wealth than they already own. This was borne out by a survey of 120 American households, each worth $25 million or more (the group boasted two billionaires, and an average net worth of $78 million), administered by Boston College's Center on Wealth and Philanthropy. The survey indicated that most respondents felt they needed approximately one fourth more money than they already possessed:

> Most of them still do not consider themselves financially secure; for that, they say, they would require on average one-quarter more wealth than they currently possess… One respondent, the heir to an enormous fortune, says that what matters most to him is his Christianity, and that his greatest aspiration is "to love the Lord, my family, and my friends." He also reports that he wouldn't feel financially secure until he had $1 billion in the bank. (Wood, 2011: 72–78)

Even after they could comfortably retire, extremely wealthy Americans often continue working. According to the author of the 2013 *Forbes* article "Why Do the Mega Rich Continue to Work?" even after they could live "…the rest of their lives on their yachts, many mega-rich professionals devote more than 40 hours a week in jobs that are often times banal and stressful." Why do these fortunate ones continue to drag through the old daily grind even when they don't need to financially? Many of the reasons they give fall under the category of "enough is never enough":

- Many mega-rich "…are dismissive of their accomplishments and it drives them to reach higher…" [I haven't reeled in enough money yet, need to keep trying.]
- Others continue to work "for posterity. Need to go out with another winner." [I haven't earned enough to garner my descendants' respect.]
- "Even when those with a cash-out sum hit their desired stash, people find themselves needing more money in order to really leave it all behind…" [I haven't made enough money yet.]

Other reasons given:

- "If you truly love what you are doing, why stop?" [Hmmm.

You're still crazy about the mind-numbing, stressful job you've endured for 40 years?]

- "People enjoy being challenged." [How about being challenged by tennis? Travel? Learning a new skill?]
- "Beach living is boring." [So... maybe volunteer? Learn how to build sailboats? Write a novel?]
- "Working keeps you young." [So, do volunteering for the Audubon Society, stone sculpting, or take up a hobby like bee keeping.]

But it's not just the super-rich who have a hard time accurately sizing up their financial conditions. According to the Pew Research Center, few Americans view themselves as wealthy regardless of their financial situations. Pew researchers, for example, found that people earning $30,000 a year thought "wealthy" meant earning at least $100,000. Conversely, people earning $100,000 felt "wealthy" meant earning at least $500,000 a year (Reeves, 2015).

The question of course, is, Why? What drives some people to overeat, "shop till they drop," and hoard until the only place at home to eat, sleep and live is a small portion of the bed not piled high with 1,000 old copies of *The New York Times*? Why would those worth $78 million plus, feel financially insecure? Why would the mega-rich retain boring, stressful jobs they don't need? Why do men like the Koch Brothers of Koch Industries – who in 2008 shared the world's single largest fortune – continue slaving for even greater wealth? If they lived 10 lifetimes Charles and David Koch would have to race like roadrunners to spend their current $95 billion.

According to psychologists, hoarding disorder, compulsive buying disorder, and eating disturbances are attempts to fill unmet emotional needs (Benson, 2008; Brown et al., 2009). But is that the whole story? Could there be other forces at work here, in addition to those considered psychological? One thing many of those suffering eating, hoarding, shopping and money disorders share in common is this: for them enough is never enough. Or, to put a finer point on it, to them enough never *feels* like enough. No matter how it complicates their lives, the act of amassing more and more is paramount.

It is the thesis of this book that although civilizations the world over have produced spectacular innovations – monumental architecture, complex mathematics, magnificent art, and the invention of writing, to name a few – civilizations have also produced several unsavory "innovations," which to the modern mind seem an inevitable part of living in civilized society.

But these unsavory innovations are not inevitable. They began around 6000 years ago in early Mesopotamia when sudden, widespread, and chronic climate change produced multigenerational starvation in certain, small isolated groups. This starvation resulted in ugly survival behaviors, such as hoarding, violent theft, inequality, treating women, children and others as chattel, etc. Over several generations these survival behaviors became crystalized in these groups, into new and fixed cultural norms.

At the same time most Mesopotamians were starving in newly formed deserts, those at the famous Tigris and Euphrates Rivers possessed enough water to remain prosperous, peaceful and socially equitable. When the violent starvation groups began intermixing with the River communities, however, the resulting hybrid population became one characterized by large-scale violence, a power elite, enslavement for most, widespread disease, and institutionalized warfare.

Large-scale architecture was invented to store hoarded food and other goods, which were produced by the enslaved masses but enjoyed primarily by the power elite. Writing was invented not for the good of humanity, but to keep track of hoarded commodities. Institutionalized warfare was invented to steal slaves, who could produce enough to fill the monumental storage containers to maximum capacity.

From Mesopotamia these cancerous cultural norms spread first to Egypt, then China, then Europe, and finally, around 200 CE, to Mexico in the New World (although many scholars disagree, it was probably the Chinese who gifted Mexico with the state; more on this later).

Today the norms first adopted by long-starving people 6000 years ago are thoroughly entrenched worldwide, giving the impression that they are inevitable. They are not. And if humanity continues to believe they are, we risk the annihilation of our own species.

When I think about my potential readers, my worst fear is they will shy away from this book because of its troubling subject matter: people living with blistering food shortages for long periods of time, and inevitably responding in freakishly bizarre ways. I say "inevitably" because on a variety of levels the brains and bodies of nutrition-deprived individuals undergo specific kinds of long-term stress. The stress, then, leads to the unorthodox behavior. My second greatest fear is that I will fail to explain clearly the process by which this psychotic behavior became crystalized into a permanent way of life that gradually, over the past 6000 years, spread like the plague throughout the world until it now threatens to annihilate us all.

This process involves not only the horrific climate change that blistered the earth 6000 years ago, but also – unfortunately – the concept "culture." Few people understand culture, or the gigantic role it plays in shaping our lives. Even those who do understand it often forget how powerful it is (I'm thinking of myself here). My hope is that at some point the ideas presented in this book might help drag our poor bedraggled species out of the sink hole we've stumbled into. The hole was not always totally dark and lonely. At one or more times in the past, "starvation culture" was a lifesaver, keeping some of our ancestors from dying out completely. In today's world, however, its only purpose is an evil one, and it's past time we pitch it out on its ear – before it crushes our species into oblivion.

Chapter 1

"Houston, We Have a Problem"

Pride

American, European, Australian, Middle Eastern and Asian countries, or "state societies," are justifiably proud of themselves. For starters, we can all boast technological prowess. Compared to smaller-scale societies and indigenous peoples of pre-Columbian North America, the Brazilian Rainforest, Australia and many other world areas, we "advanced" societies are techno wizards who fly to the moon, harness the energy and light of the sun, and communicate in the blink of an eye over vast distances. State societies are political pioneers, too, creators of the world's first large-scale democracies, in which average people, through the ballot box, have a say in how they are governed.

State societies also take great pride in their material wealth and magnanimity. On a regular basis the US sends giant ships bulging with doctors and other medical professionals to help the sick the world over; I know this first-hand, because my nephew Ike oversaw the embarkation routine at each port of call for one such ship. When disaster hits either at home or abroad, state societies the world over often reach into their pockets and rush headlong into troubled areas to lend a helping hand.

So, we state societies can pat ourselves on the back for more than one sterling-silver quality. However, when thoughts of our national imperfections ooze up from the depths of our cerebral cortexes, we often quickly stuff them back down again. Since few of us like to dwell on these national warts, I'll offer only the following short list: perpetual warfare, high rates of crime and violence, human trafficking, high rates of rape, incest, poverty and physical, mental and child abuse; drug abuse, anomie and social inequality. Although these rotten qualities darken the lights of all state societies, they darken some more than others. This has been true for the past 6000 years, i.e., since the first "state" societies arose in Mesopotamia.

So exactly how and why did our warts originate? Did all our ancestors possess them? No; before around 4000 BCE they plagued few societies, if any. One clue about where our warts came from lies in this singular fact: most of our warty behavior bears a striking resemblance to that of people living for generations on the edge of starvation. More on this later. For now, we need to put the "state society" under a microscope, because it's with the state that our troubles seem to have arisen.

The State Defined (Snore, Snore, Zzzzz)

The word "state" makes me itchy. The word is annoyingly fuzzy and indistinct. Not only does "state" spill over with multiple meanings, these meanings tend to be murky and blurry. Mostly they're murky because they refer to things you can't touch, smell or taste. Even murkier is the kind of state we're interested in here: "the state" as your way of life if you live in a "country". "Well, duh!" you say, "Everyone lives in a country, so what other way of life is there!" True. But back in the day, we didn't live in these things we call countries. In the past, no one lived in countries because countries did not exist.

Did Columbus discover countries in 1492 when he bumbled into the Americas? No. When we all hung out in caves, did countries exist? No, they did not. Countries, in other words – the idea of them – had to be invented. And it turns out that before countries were invented, life was dramatically different. In fact, the difference is like apples and oranges. Or, better, like shiny red apples and rotten brown oranges.

To best understand the country/state, let's drop a country next to an indigenous society and compare the two. Indigenous societies still follow the ways of their distant ancestors, and most of them still live on the lands these ancestors inhabited. They are "tribal" societies. Indigenous peoples "...still retain their cultural heritage" and they still follow their ancient "cosmogonic myths and ancestral values systems..." (Rival, 2001). For our comparison, we'll tap modern Americans and compare them to the early twentieth-century Eskimos, now called "Inuit." Although the Inuit live in the country/state of Canada, until recently Canada took a hands-off approach to the group, allowing them to live their ancient way of life with no interference from Canada, the state. We'll therefore compare American life to the traditional Inuit life that existed before state interference.

Working a "Job"

When comparing Americans and Inuit people, a big difference jumps out at you right off the bat: the Inuit don't work "jobs" in the American, British, Canadian, or Australian sense of the word. Unless Americans inherit money from Aunt Millie or Uncle Joe, or own their own business, they depend on getting salaries in exchange for work they do for someone (or something) else. Although most Americans hold down salaried jobs, they're not guaranteed to get jobs they like – or even of landing a job at all. What's more, they rarely have any say over how much they'll get paid for the job, or over what their work conditions will be. Also, for no reason whatsoever, their employer can dump them – sometimes with no advance notice at all. "Clean out your desk, and leave by the end of the day." Bam.

Despite all the above ugly slave-like conditions attached to American jobs, most Americans have no other way to survive. Unless they take a salaried job, they find themselves dining in soup kitchens or out of garbage bins, and sleeping in homeless camps, abandoned buildings or cardboard boxes in the park. Some jobs, however, make soup kitchens and cardboard-box homes actually look good. For example, since they're not even given regular bathroom breaks, workers at certain US chicken processing plants actually wear diapers to work (Associated

Press, 2016). My guess is, some of these workers might begin to think of garbage-bin dinners and tent homes as preferable to chicken processing.

Unlike Americans and people in other state societies, Inuit people didn't need jobs to eat well, or own a home. So if they didn't work jobs, how did they spend their days? Most of the men sallied forth in groups to "grocery shop," or bring home the bacon, so to speak. Although Inuit hunting groups were made up mostly of men, women also sometimes hunted. After the hunt, the hunters divided the game, and each family walked away with an equal share of the meat. It didn't matter who actually wrestled the bacon to the ground, everyone got a fair share of it. While men did most of the hunting, women did the construction work, including constructing housing, clothes, food, beds, meals and so forth.

Although Inuit work could be arduous, it was also satisfying. Ironically, much of the work the Inuit did to survive, Americans now do for pleasure: hunting, fishing, cooking, weaving, potting and a whole host of other craft hobbies are what Americans do outside of their slave wage jobs, to relax. In contrast to the Inuit, many Americans find their wage jobs not only dissatisfying, but actually painful. The misery felt by many American workers is humorously portrayed in the 2018 dark comedy series "Corporate":

> "Look at these people," [the character Matt] observes as he and Jake walk through a row of [office] cubicles and try to diagnose their inhabitants. "Is everyone at this company clinically depressed?"
>
> "Everyone here's hanging by a thread," Jake replies. "They could snap at any moment."
>
> "These were all children once. Happy, innocent children," Matt adds as the camera pans over workers' forlorn faces. One woman stares blankly into space. A man's forehead rests

> dejectedly on his desk. Another looks shiftily to his right as he takes in a deep sniff of a permanent marker. "Now look at them. How did this happen?"

Not only did the creators of "Corporate" work for corporations themselves, they also interviewed other corporate employees:

> Beyond basing the show on their own experiences, the creators did their research, interviewing people who worked for massive companies like Amazon and Google. "It turns out it's even worse than we thought and everyone's in hell," Ingebretson says, matter-of-factly. (Wilstein, 2018)

Snobs

Another difference between countries, or state societies, and people like the Inuit is this: countries are stuffed full of snobs, while traditional societies like the Inuit's generally are not. Snobs are people who think they're better than you – and your country (state society) agrees that they are. Americans don't like to think they have a snob system (aka "social hierarchy," "social status system," "class system"), but take garbage collectors and surgeons, for example. Do sanitary engineers and surgeons typically swill beer and martinis together at the same parties? No. Would Donald Trump invite most Americans to lunch at Mar a Lago? Probably not. In contrast, Inuit snobs are scarce as Arctic alligators, with any one Inuit being considered as good as any other.

Top Snobs Running the Show

Here's another thing Americans don't like to think is true of America: in countries, at the very top of the pecking order, sits a small group of people that secretly runs the country. Many Americans might not like to think they're run by a power elite, but former President Jimmy Carter knows better. In 2015 Carter declared that the US is now less a democracy than an oligarchy (a country run by a small group of people) (Schwartz, 2015). Just one sign of this: Congress increasingly thumbs its nose at the American voter, obeying instead a small ruling elite that hides in the shadows behind closed doors and pays Congress to do their bidding.

In contrast, no Inuit or group of Inuit held power over the entire Inuit community, and the Inuit would never freely have given away their personal power to a president, governor, mayor or work boss. Yes, they chose someone to lead their hunts, but that person might easily change depending on the year, the season, or the hunt. For example, whoever knew most about walruses led walrus hunts, and whoever knew most about polar bears led the bear hunts.

Going to Prison

Another big difference between state societies and other people: state societies keep prisons – ugly places that slam you away from the world for up to years. States pay people to do nothing all day long but catch you and drop you into these ugly places, if that's where the state wants you. The Inuit, on the other hand, had neither prisons nor law enforcement personnel. They didn't need them. In traditional Inuit society, the desire to keep one's good name with neighbors was enough to keep people honest.

In sum, if you live in a state society, you are privy to a "special" kind of life, dominated by a power elite that parades around in the open (in places like Saudi Arabia, China and North Korea), or lurks in the shadows (in most of Europe, Australia and North America). Whether they parade around openly or hide in the shadows, your elite "owns" law enforcement bogeymen who can club you over the head and pitch you out of circulation the minute you dare poke at them, the elite (this, for example, was the fate in 2012 and 2013 of many leaders of America's Occupy Wall Street movement).

Over time, the nature of power elites has changed. In the days of kings and queens, power-elite groups consisted of royals and church bigwigs. Now, however, as it was in the Age of the Robber Barons at the end of the nineteenth and start of the twentieth centuries, the American power elite is a fistful of mega-wealthy Americans who keep a larger group of plain-wealthy folks happy by giving them special tax cuts and other treats. These plain-wealthy tax-cut recipients we'll call "the henchmen of the power elite." Unlike the power elite and their henchmen, to eat and keep a roof over their heads most other Americans slave away for masters who might or might not toss them enough food, shelter and dignity to keep body and soul together.

The First States

By now you should have a skeletal understanding of the state. But to really know the beast you must meet the mother of all states, the first one, the one I think gave birth to all the rest. You must also understand how and why ancient, near-utopian nonstate communities suddenly jerked into the world's first cities and city-states, which archaeologists now know were not the bright, shining beacons on a hill your fifth-grade teacher told you they were, but actually hideous places stuffed full of disease, violence and slavery. At the core of the infant state was its power elite and their use of violence to silence the people they lived among. All else about the state – social hierarchy, poverty, police/law enforcement, armies, wars, slavery, economic surpluses, taxes, division of labor, physical violence, runaway crime – flows from this one element: the existence of a violent power elite.

Where did these first violent top-snobs come from? The theory most in favor currently is one laid down by a man named Robert Caneiro. But as we'll soon see, there are plenty of holes in Caneiro's way of looking at the issue.

A Major Theory of the Origin of the State

Sociocultural systems are all different, and it's virtually impossible to turn one into another. Take the English and the French, for example. In spite of living cheek to jowl for millennia, the English are still solidly English, and the French decidedly French. On the one hand heavy meat pies, on the other, fine French cuisine. Stolid and stately London versus whimsical "gay" Paree. So how and why, in antiquity, would comparatively small peaceful groups morph into giant violent ones – virtually overnight?

One of the most popular answers to the question "Why did the state first rear its ugly head?" is Robert Caneiro's "circumscription" theory (Caneiro, 1970). I like to call it Caneiro's "squirrels-and-nuts" theory, since it's based on the idea that when food and other resources grow scarce, everyone begins to wage war to steal from neighbors, punch the neighbors into slavery, and then punish the slaves into producing a surplus – like squirrels gathering nuts for a blistering hard winter. According to Caneiro this is how the first state began in 4000 BCE. But Caneiro can't be right. Yes, some nonstate societies today wage war to snatch things from their neighbors, but none of them try to conquer and enslave their neighbors:

> [T]he main flaw of Carneiro's original theory of state formation is that it implicitly assumes that every community dreamt to conquer its neighboring communities. We test[ed] the presence of various types of warfare (such as conquest warfare, land acquisition warfare, and plunder warfare) in societies with different degrees of political centralization. Quantitative cross-cultural tests reveal a rather strong correlation between political complexity and the presence of conquest warfare, suggesting that conquest warfare was virtually absent among independent communities. (Zinkina et al., 2016: 187)

Also, if institutionalized warfare didn't exist before 4000 BCE (and most scholars now believe it didn't), how might any group of people morph in as little as 100 years from peaceniks into people who not only understood conquest warfare, but were aces at waging it, and seemed even to blindly accept it? Evidence does indeed suggest that the jump from peaceful peoples at the Tigris and Euphrates rivers to brutal, violent warlike ones, did indeed explode in as little as 100 years. Our best evidence suggests that before 4000 BCE the peaceful peoples living at the Tigris probably couldn't even imagine using hunting weapons to hurt other human beings, let alone kill them. So, they certainly had no practiced skill at using weapons to coerce or hurt others. Neither do we have evidence for human slavery at the Tigris River before around 4000 BCE.

My Theory

It is the thesis of this book that the bad stuff began when an ancient group of people, after starving for generations, teetered on the brink of extinction. What saved them was this: their physically strongest male began violently stealing food out of the mouths of everyone else in his community. This alpha male then doled out his leftover scraps to a small group of starving, suck-up henchmen willing to do his bidding, no questions asked. Although as a result most in Alpha's group died of starvation, his me-first move actually saved the group from total extinction. The biggest down side, however, is that a new way of life was created, one ugly as a hobgoblin fattened on human-flesh, one based on the enslavement of most by a few. This way of life, predicated as it was on fear-based, violent taking behavior, spread like wildfire – through violent conquest. In a nutshell this is how large cities, countries, the state, and "civilization" began.

This theory of how the state began takes into account two new recent pieces of evidence. The first is the 3900 BCE "5.9 Kiloyear Event," possibly one of the most devastating climate events ever to take place in the Holocene Epoch, the geological time period we're living in now. The second is that archaeologists are beginning to admit that far from what many of us were taught in school, the rise in Mesopotamia of the first cities, of civilization, was not a giant leap forward for humanity, but actually a few giant leaps backward. More on both these new bits of evidence, in later chapters.

As I suggested earlier, I'm actually allergic to the word "state." Since the state was birthed by people who lived on the hellish brink of extinction long enough to invent a brand-new way of life, one based on their particular deadly dilemma – starvation – my term for the state is "starvation culture." When I use the term starvation culture throughout the remainder of this book, please know that I am using it as a synonym for "country," "state," and "civilization."

Chapter 2

These People Aren't Pretty

To hunger, nothing is sacred ~ Sorokin, 1975

In this book I will show that Americans and other state-society people behave much like people who've starved for long periods of time. I plan to show that our starvation-like behavior is what shakes us apart from the world's peaceful, egalitarian societies, none of whom act like starving people. Anthropologists have looked into the behavior of several starving or food-anxious tribal societies, including the Kalauna of New Guinea, the Gurage of Ethiopia, the Siriono of Bolivia, the Tikopians of the South Pacific, and the Ik of Uganda. Others have written about nineteenth- and twentieth-century famines in Russia, China, Ukraine and other state societies, and if you sift through the frightening facts about government repression, nutritional deprivation, and mortality rates, you catch bits and pieces about bizarre shifts in social behavior in such societies.

In what follows I'll talk less about China, Russia and other states, however, than about indigenous societies, since this book is about how starving indigenous groups gave rise to today's state societies. In many ways, however, starving states behave much like starving nonstates. In both, people's eating behavior becomes wacky, people hoard things (especially food), they spend much of their time scouring their surroundings for food, they steal food, they become violent, and if famine waltzes on long enough, their entire social order falls apart.

As you might expect, how badly people behave depends on how long they've been starving. According to anthropologist Robert Dirks starving groups shuffle through three different phases. When food first becomes scarce and the whiff of famine hangs in the air, people become revved up and extremely sociable. They can't do enough for each other. This is stage one. In stage two, when food becomes even scarcer, people "shove the car in reverse" so to speak: hide in their homes and avoid anyone outside their immediate family. It's in this stage that hoarding, theft and violence begin to rear their ugly heads. In the final stage, stage three, when food is almost non-existent, even the family breaks apart and people do whatever it takes to get food into their own individual mouths – whether it means selling the baby to the highest bidder or kicking Grandpa to the curb. In this stage, says Dirks, culture ceases to exist. "For the time being... culture disappears, leaving an essentially bestial nature..." (Dirks, 1980: 31).

Dirks calls these three stages "Alarm," "Resistance" and "Exhaustion." In what follows we'll drop each of these stages under a microscope to see what people do to each other as the starvation process marches on toward Armageddon.

Starvation Stage 1: "Alarm"

In the first, or Alarm stage, people get wired. There's "intense interaction," and "abnormal excitement." People are drawn together like flies to honey, and are just lovely to each other: sharing food and cooperating like there's no tomorrow. At the same time, they can fly off the handle seemingly over nothing, and are nervous and restless. They have a tendency to wander, to pick up and take off for parts unknown. "Mass emigration is often diagnostic of famine," says Dirks. If state-society people riot or revolt, they do it now, since this is the only stage in which they have enough energy to make much of a fuss; in the final two stages they're too spent to do much of anything but hunt for food – or sit quietly dying.

Starvation Stage 2: "Resistance"

> Mr Kim and his wife... described the sound of famine: like frogs or mosquitoes in the night, the children crying with hunger (Fahy, 2011). [The Kims were refugees who had escaped from North Korea.]

As hunger continues to sink its talons deeper into a group, people's behavior shifts dramatically. They turn from racing around like nervous ninnies to hiding at home, hoping no one notices they're too tired to till the fields or punch the clock at work. Social ties weaken. Generosity and altruism fly out the window. People begin to save everything, including their own bodily energy, and they don't do much else but trudge around looking for food.

In Stage 2, people are still sharing food but only within the immediate family; friends and more distant relatives suddenly drop off the sharing list. Raymond Firth, the anthropologist who lived on the island of Tikopia in the South Pacific when Tikopians were in this stage, says people stopped serving food to kinfolk who dropped by; relatives would hustle over expecting dinner, but would wait for it in vain (Firth, 1959: 82). Likewise, the Siriono of Bolivia shared nothing with anyone outside their immediate families. The Siriono survived by hunting and gathering, but game is scarce in their forests, their weapons are rudimentary (bows and arrows), and they don't store food. As a result, when Holmsberg lived among them they were constantly hungry and anxious about food (Holmsberg, 1969).

Among the Gurage of Ethiopia, custom dictated that you share food with friends and neighbors, but the Gurage skirted this rule by never eating in public – where people could see the food and demand their just due. Like the Siriono, the Gurage were constantly nervous about the specter of starvation, which for them lurked around every corner – the result of their being bullied, raided and ransacked for generations by their thuggish neighbors (Shack, William 1971). In Ireland too, community spirit hemorrhaged during the infamous Irish potato famine; "[H]ardship and hunger broke the communal spirit of the people, who became preoccupied with the struggle to survive and lost their sympathy for each other" (Edwards et al., 1957: 434). And during WWII starving war prisoners often formed small "family" units that hoarded food and shared only within their group. As you might expect, in the long run these prisoners came out better off than those who didn't form similar kinds of support groups (Dirks, 1980).

It's in stage two that eating disorders appear. The Siriono wolfed down their food, and to avoid sharing it ate at night under the cover of darkness, or snuck into the forest to eat (Holmsberg, 1969). Like anorexics, the Gurage ate appallingly little, and both they and the Kalauna underfed their children. When anthropologists studied them, Kaluana children were on the verge of malnourishment (Shack, Dorothy 2012). Even though the Kalauna grew yams, taro, bananas and sweet potatoes, kept pigs and also hunted and fished, they were nevertheless nervous about food. Michael Young, the anthropologist who studied them, suspects they'd been blistered by frequent famines due to drought, hurricanes, insect pests and heavy rains (Young, 1986).

Although the Gurage typically ate like birds – at any meal they consumed "slight handfuls, to nibbles, to hardly any" – at certain festivals they ate "to the point of glut" (Shack, William 2012). After a few centuries of being sliced and diced by their bellicose neighbors, the Gurage had learned their lesson: look plump and prosperous and your enemies will come knocking at your door looking to plunder your wealth; look skeletal and they won't bother you.

The Kalauna, who believed in a curse in which people die from gorging on food, used magic spells to weaken their appetites (Dirks, 1994). Unlike Westerners, who tell children that to grow big and strong they need to clean their plates, Kalauna parents tell children it's eating like birds that will make them big and strong. Among the Kalauna, the most-feared curse made them uncontrollably hungry, forcing them to steal food or eat so piggishly that their stomachs would burst apart (Russell, 2005).

During stage two, families begin hoarding and hiding food. The Gurage grew tons more food than they could possibly eat, and buried most of it in deep storage pits covered over with garden refuse. During China's famine of 1958–61 – one of the worst in human history – people hoarded food very carefully, since if Mao's henchmen caught them committing this most heinous of sins, they'd be punished severely, or even executed (Becker, 2013).

Not surprisingly, starving people's eyes light up over almost nothing but food. According to an eighty-year-old Irish potato-famine survivor, during the famine "Sport and pastimes disappeared. Poetry, music and dancing stopped. They lost and forgot them all and when the times improved in other respects, these things never returned as they had been" (Edwards et al., 1957: 435). Among starving people sex disorders are common as flies at spring picnics. The Siriono enjoyed very little sex – except when there was a glut of food, at which time they also engaged in a glut of sex (Holmsberg, 1969: 255). In order to keep from starving, Ik women exchanged sex (with non-Ik neighbors) for food (Turnbull, 1972), and in the 1919–21 Russian famine prostitution became a national pastime.

In starvation's stage two, people begin to fight over and steal food. Forbidden to cook at home, Chinese famine peasants from 1959 to 1962 lined up twice a day for food cooked in communal kitchens, fighting each other as they waited, and with young people shoving their elders out of line (Becker, 2013). During Russia's 1919–21 famine "hundreds of bands" roamed the countryside, robbing and pillaging villages, trains and small towns (Sorokin, 1975: 138, 140). The Siriono regularly fought each other over food, and when Ik men were asked to carry government food back to their villages, the food never made it, since the men stopped and gobbled it up on the way home (Turnbull, 1972).

Starvation Stage 3: "Exhaustion"

The big bang that tips the scales during the final stage of starvation is the collapse of the family. In the Exhaustion stage it's everyone for herself, others be damned – including Grandpa, Grandma, and junior wailing in his crib from stomach-cramping hunger pains. During the 1959–62 Chinese famine, husbands stole food coupons from their wives, parents stole food from their children, and cases were reported of "sons beating or even killing their own mothers" (Becker, 2013). This kind of family breakdown blistered all Dirks' stage-three groups, and in countries as diverse as Austria and Uganda.

In stage three, people too young, old, sick or disabled to hunt, gather or otherwise lay their hands on food are summarily abandoned. Among the Ik both old and young alike were left to die, and the Siriono regularly abandoned both the elderly and people too sick to work. Although in most starving groups the elderly are first to go, China reverses this trend; during most of its famines – and over the centuries China's had several – first to be left to meet their maker are young daughters (Becker, 2013). In Russia during the 1918–21 famine children were often abandoned or sold (Sorokin, 1975: 114), and those who today escape North Korea also speak about children being abandoned by starving parents (a major famine skewered North Korea in 1995, after the country had already slogged through decades of "undernutrition") (Fahy, 2011).

Cannibalism swept through China and Russia alike during their twentieth-century famines. Sorokin says that in Russia cannibalism was "an ordinary occurrence," with Russians excavating and eating corpses or even murdering and then consuming neighbors, friends and relatives (Sorokin, 1975). Waxing poetic, Sorokin opines that "...starvation mercilessly rips off the 'social' garments from man and shows him as a naked animal, on the naked earth" (Sorokin, 1975: 137).

In twentieth-century famine-ravaged China too, cannibalism was widespread:

> There are enough reports from different parts of the country to make it clear that the practice of cannibalism was not restricted to any one region, class or nationality. Peasants not only ate the flesh of the dead, they also sold it, and they killed and ate children, both their own and those of others. (Becker, 2013)

To avoid consuming their own children, some Chinese resorted to "swap and eat," a bizarre practice involving killing your own child, and swapping its body with the body of someone else's child.

But cannibalism kicks up its ugly heels in Western states too. In Ukraine in 1932–33, while famine was claiming the lives of over 5 million people, some Ukrainians were busy selling human flesh in public markets. After the crisis ended, trials were held for over 300 cases of cannibalism. And at Treblinka, the infamous Nazi death camp in Poland, a British rescue worker noticed that roughly one tenth of the bodies of the dead had chunks missing from the backs of their thighs. The worker reportedly witnessed a prisoner pull out a knife, clip out a chunk of the leg from a corpse, and pop it into his mouth (Becker, 2013).

After they're kicked out of the house, children in some famine-blitzed societies form into gangs that roam the streets, or depending on a group's location – the forests, mountains or valleys, scouting for food. Such child gangs formed in Russia, Uganda, and the Netherlands alike. Children begged or stole food, using violence if necessary. More on such child gangs later on, when we take a closer look at the Ik of Uganda, one of the few if not only stage-three indigenous groups whose famine behavior has been placed under a microscope and then written about.

If you're grinding your teeth now over the hideous nature of the human species, here's something to lighten your mood: in all starving groups studied, certain people react not with self-centeredness and violence, but with generosity and kindness (Dirks, 1980: 21). We don't know what percentage of people react humanely, but the fact that some do is good enough for me.

One last word about famine's final "Exhaustion" stage: Most people who reach it are too exhausted to do much of anything but sit or sleep. During China's 1959–62 famine one person's office "often checked the staff and told people to rest to prevent the entire workforce from collapsing" (Becker, 2013). In Uganda Colin Turnbull watched one small group sit close together for three solid days without speaking, gazing out over a valley below them. In Russian famine districts families huddled on the tops of huge stoves and hibernated like bears in an almost continuous winter sleep called *loijka* (Dirks, 1980: 28), and at the end of the Irish potato famine rescue workers found people huddled together in corners of their huts, so still they were taken for dead (Dirks, 1980: 30).

Getting Down into the Belly of the Beast: The Ik

Although enlightening, the above information is admittedly sketchy. It would be nice to describe in a bit more detail a few indigenous groups suffering through starvation's final stage, i.e., groups resembling the starving 4000-BCE groups who created the first civilizations in Mesopotamia. Such studies, however, are scarce as hen's teeth. Tons have been written about the physical effects of starvation, but few have tackled the task of coldly and clinically observing the behavior of people deep in the starvation beast's belly. And this makes sense. Who wants to coldly and clinically observe people in the hellish depths of starvation? Most of us want to help, not stand by and gawk. And few of us want to add to the misery of starving people by publishing information about the ways they've abused one another.

The only in-depth study of a long-starving, stage-three indigenous group I'm aware of is Colin Turnbull's fieldwork among the Ik of Uganda. In the mid-1960s Turnbull lived for a year and a half with this African group, one that had starved for at least three generations in a row – long enough for only the oldest among them to remember a time when there was enough food, and a time when people behaved decently and with kindness toward others. In his 1972 book *The Mountain People* Turnbull documented in detail the social decay and bizarre behavior of the Ik, and it has been said that "...no other book has painted a darker picture of the wicked force of famine in extinguishing social relations" (Willersley and Meinert, 2017).

The Ik (pronounced Eek) are a small isolated group perched on the border between northeastern Uganda, Sudan and Kenya in central Africa. They're also known as the Tueso, but to them the latter is a pejorative term, and will not be used in this book. The Ik live on "...an enormous range of jagged, wildly irregular mountains... reaching upward like gnarled, knotted fingers, ...a lunar landscape" (Turnbull, 1972: 40). According to Turnbull the Ik are short people – about five feet on average. Under their dark tans (from long days in the sun) their skin is "light red in color," and "when they moved it was with the quick, short steps that distinguish a mountain people from those of the plains" (Turnbull, 1972: 55–56). He describes at least one Ik as having blue eyes.

The Ik are an isolated people. Some of the mountain paths Turnbull was forced to maneuver to reach Ik villages were so treacherous that by the time he reached the first village he'd torn holes in his shirt and pants from hugging the rock face bordering his trail. From his path "it must have been a good fifteen-hundred-foot drop down into Kenya, and possibly two thousand... [M]y left leg was bruised and cut from scraping it along the rock face, to which I now unashamedly clung with both hands" (Turnbull, 1972: 46–47).

In the mid-1960s the 20 or so Ik villages were laid out in a string running northwest to southeast between Uganda's Kidepo National Park in the north and its Timu Forest in the south. Each village huddled on top of a hill, with views of wooded valleys below. Villages contained as few as 10 and as many as 50 family compounds. Describing one of the first Ik villages he finally stumbled into, Turnbull writes:

> Nawedo was given its name because it is always in the clouds... The ground was damp with mist, yet ironically it was scorched brown. Nearby fields... were withered and fruitless. But there was the village, a cluster of fifteen or so circular houses with mudded walls and conical thatched roofs... Some of the houses were no more than three feet from the edge of the cliff... (Turnbull, 1972: 48)

According to Turnbull, in the mid-1960s the Ik numbered around 1300. To stop neighbors from stealing their stuff, Ik homes were hemmed in by tall stockades – even though no one had much to steal. Although Turnbull did most of his research in the Ik town of Pirre, which lies in the far north of Ikland, he also observed life in five other Ik villages (Heine, 1985: 5).

By the time Turnbull got to them, the Ik had become "a people on the brink of utter starvation and extinction, a people whose depravity Turnbull described in stark detail" (Grinker, 2000). A humdinger of a drought had killed their crops, and although game roamed freely below them in Kidepo National Park and south in the Timu Forest, the government forbade the Ik to hunt or kill them. Turnbull tried to alert the Ugandan government to the dire situation in Ikland, but to no avail. Part of the problem was that Ik men strong enough to walk were charged with carrying government food back to the villages, but the food was scarfed down on the trail before it could ever reach the villagers left behind.

Before his first contact with the Ik, Turnbull heard they were going hungry (but not that they were dying of starvation), so he packed his Land Rover with a substantial load of grain, sugar, rice, beans and other food to distribute. None of these supplies, however, reached the Ik, since they were "liberated" by Atum, the Ik man who would eventually become Turnbull's main informant.

Another part of the problem was political. In the mid-1960s, Uganda had just won its independence from the UK, and its new president, Apollo Milton Obote, essentially thumbed his nose at the Ik's Karamoja region, which was "not regarded as important for the development of the nation" (Willersley and Meinert, 2017). Meanwhile, the resultant Ik-on-Ik savagery that Turnbull witnessed can hardly be overstated. Children and oldsters were unceremoniously left to rot and die, and the photos Turnbull snapped show elderly Ik looking for all the world like the skeletal humans starved to death by the Nazis at concentration camps such as Auschwitz and Buchenwald.

The Ik regularly stole from the weakest among them, even to the point of yanking food directly out of the mouths of the sick, the elderly, and children. Turnbull's Ik were understandably obsessed with food and eating; to them, nothing else seemed to matter. They described sex as about as enjoyable as a good bowel movement. Actually, Turnbull did find one other thing that almost always snagged their undivided attention: the sight of someone else suffering. The only thing other than food that gave the Ik pleasure – that made them smile and even laugh – was watching someone else suffer pain or humiliation, or both.

When the Ik stumbled onto large quantities of food, instead

of sharing with others (who were also starving, remember) they gorged until vomiting. Since many of the elderly skeletons were too weak from hunger to walk, they got from point A to point B by crawling, or by scooting along on their bottoms. A game enjoyed by Ik children was to knock the elderly down whenever they attempted, in their weakened condition, to stand up on two feet.

By the way, Turnbull makes it clear – and we should make it clear here too: any human group suffering the conditions heaped upon the Ik, for as long as the Ik suffered them, would have reacted as egregiously as the Ik did. As we'll see later on, severe long-term hunger and malnutrition plays havoc with human mental and physical health, and it's a mistake to think that you, your people, or any other human group would react any less horrendously to this kind of scourge than the Ik did in the mid-1960s.

Twenty years after Turnbull's sorry sojourn with the Ik, Ikland seems to have recovered some of its equilibrium. By 1985 the Red Cross had moved in, and many villages now enjoyed schools. Bernd Heine, who studied the Ik during February and March of 1985, says the population was at least double the 1300 figure Turnbull threw out in the mid-1960s. Heine seems to find the Ik about as normal as any other human group, reporting no anti-social, violent, or otherwise bizarre behavior, and he actually goes so far as to accuse Turnbull of projecting his own anger onto the Ik, and lifting his information not from the Ik but from non-Ik people, who Heine contends were living in large numbers in the mid-1960s with the Ik. At any rate, Heine's 1985 description of the Ik suggests that by this time the group had bounced back, to one extent or another, from the pit they'd fallen into in the 1960s. At least some of the values, morays, norms and behaviors of their new school teachers, Red Cross workers, and people from other nearby healthy communities were probably rubbing off – onto younger Ik especially.

For his refusal to quit an excruciatingly difficult stint of anthropological fieldwork, Turnbull was later demonized by his colleagues. A cadre of anthropologists accused him of slandering the Ik and of getting much of his information about them wrong. Anthropologist Frederik Barth led the attack, publishing a scathing 1974 article in anthropology's premier American journal, *Current Anthropology*: "On Responsibility and Humanity: Calling a Colleague to Account" (Barth, 1974).

Fifty years later, and as a result of this storm of controversy over Turnbull's dealings with the Ik, researchers Rane Willerslev and Lotte Meinert waltzed into Ikland to stage a "Turnbull intervention." The idea was to read horrifying passages from Turnbull's *The Mountain People,* out loud, in order to observe Ik reactions. Although the authors admitted they had expected the Ik to vehemently deny Turnbull's revolting descriptions of their ancestors, the Ik did not. They replied that their antecedents had probably behaved just as Turnbull said they had, since at the time in question they were starving to death. One older woman even admitted that she herself had suffered through times of severe famine and had seen toddlers abandoned to appalling fates:

> I have had many experiences of hunger. First when I was a very young child. It was a terrible hunger. I stayed with my grandparents and we went to the bush to search for food. We had nothing to give to a child of that age (she points to a small child around 1–2 years), so we had to abandon the child in the bush and a hyena ate it. We went around for one week without eating anything. Only those who were already strong survived.

Willerslev and Meinert concluded that the Ik had probably spent decades if not longer shifting in and out of famine, and had probably always reacted according to which state they were in at the time – feast or famine. It's worth noting

> that when these two researchers visited Ikland in 2017 they discovered many of the younger Ik women attending "local protestant churches" on a regular basis. I'd be willing to bet my bank account that these young women were busily soaking up many of the values, morays, beliefs and norms one generally finds in such churches (Willerslev and Meinert, 2017).

As one might expect, since the Ik had probably been starving for decades by the time Turnbull met them, they were obsessed with food and eating. For them all pleasures faded into obscurity when placed next to any kind of food, and many did whatever it took to eat, including harming and even murdering their own brothers, sisters, parents and children. Although not to the same extent, many Americans too are obsessed with food. The US is plagued with a variety of eating disorders from obesity, bulimia, anorexia and binge eating disorder (BED), to widespread terror at the thought of being much meatier than a match stick. According to the National Association of Anorexia Nervosa and Associated Disorders, at least 30 million Americans suffer from eating disorders ("Eating Disorder Statistics," 2017). Most indigenous societies, on the other hand, do not generally suffer from such afflictions.

While the Ik stole from the weakest among them, Americans, too, steal from their weakest – by abusing their elderly, ill, poor, disabled, women, children and homeless, stealing from them the right to live normal, healthy lives. While the Ik hoarded food, Americans hoard possessions and money (their supply lines to food). For most of their short, miserable lives, the Ik waltzed around in gangs headed by their strongest males, and whether they admit it or not, Americans too live under the thumbs of a small group of powerful elites, most of them male. Unlike Americans and the Ik, indigenous peoples generally don't "steal candy from babies," nor do they meekly allow well-muscled males to push them around.

Just like the long-starving Ik, Americans too violently steal what doesn't belong to them – not only through plain old theft, but also through rape, incest, murder, "regime change," and warfare. America and other state societies go to war as regularly as your heart beats in your chest. Most state societies keep standing armies. In contrast, indigenous peoples generally do not take what doesn't belong to them, or keep standing armies.

Ik fathers regularly abandoned their families, and many American fathers too abandon their families. Some Americans become "deadbeat dads," falling flat when it comes to coughing up court-ordered child support. In contrast, indigenous fathers generally do not abandon their wives or children.

In short, more than they resemble healthy people like the Inuit of Canada, the Nubians of East Africa, the Kadar of southwest India, or the beautiful Semai of the Malay Peninsula, Americans and other starvation-culture peoples resemble the unfortunate, unhealthy, and long-starving Ik. Although many Americans admit that as a nation they have their faults, they nevertheless assume the rest of the world behaves as badly as (or worse than) they themselves do. Nothing could be further from the truth. Not all human groups are obsessed with food, or abuse their weak. Nor do all hoard, steal, abandon children, keep armies, or practice warfare. What's more, it's not normal to obsess over food, abuse the weak, hoard, steal, abandon children, or go to war as predictably as winter follows summer.

Although several healthy human groups are left on the planet, I've chosen four – the Semai of Malaysia, the Mbuti of central Africa, the Inuit of Canada, and the !Kung of south Africa to demonstrate what "normal" human behavior looks like. These four societies are proof positive that living with starvation, state-society sorrows is not an inevitable part of the human condition. As we'll see in the next chapter, while we in state societies live like abused children, those in many of the world's hidden-away, indigenous tribal societies live like kings and queens. The renowned anthropologist Marshall Sahlins says about our indigenous peoples that, "even when relegated to the most undesirable environments, [they are] 'the original affluent society'" (Scott, 2013).

Chapter 3

I'm Not Happy, Why Are They?

In this chapter, we'll take a look at six different world peoples scattered over three continents: North America, Asia and Africa. Two of these peoples are sick, and the other four aren't. We'll compare Americans, the Ik, the Semai, the Mbuti, the Inuit, and the !Kung. While Americans suffer under the iron fist of the state, these five indigenous groups do not. The Ik, however, were pummeled for generations by another bogeyman – severe, long-term starvation – a scourge that for a while left them as dead and devastated as a turkey carved and sliced for Sunday dinner.

In contrast to the Ik, when they were first studied by anthropologists 50–100 years ago, the Semai, Mbuti, !Kung and Inuit were some of the happiest, most peaceful, most egalitarian cultures left on earth. Over the intervening years, however, to a greater or lesser extent, they too have been wounded by the state societies surrounding them. The "stories" that follow compare Americans with these five indigenous groups before they were stung by the cuts, scars and bruises inflicted upon them by the state. Story themes include entertainment, violence (or lack of it), children, sharing, hoarding and the elderly.

Entertainment

Entertainment among the Mbuti

It was honey season in the forest, and for the Mbuti days were filled with singing and games. Mammoth vines were slung high into trees, and Masamba and the other young people leapt, somersaulted and swung through the green air from one vine to another. When a vine broke, it was swept up and used for tug of war games. The sun flickered through the high trees and dropped light that dimpled everyone's arms and shoulders as the men strained on their end of the vine against the women on the other end.

When the men seemed to be gaining ground, Asofalinda, her dark-brown eyes shining with mischief, left her line, raced to the men's side, and began teasing and flirting with Kenge, who consequently found it difficult to concentrate on what he was doing. Cheering, the women gained ground. (The men were not above using the same wily maneuvers on the women when circumstances called for it.)

At dusk the Dance of the Honeybees began. As the men's dance line curled and snaked through the camp around the central fire, the men pretended to be searching for honey, craning their necks this way and that, as if looking for bees. Meanwhile, in the dimming light the women's line wove itself around the tall trees at the edge of the camp. The women, pretending to be bees, buzzed softly and provocatively, while the men, looking innocent, pretended to hear only, not see them.

Finally, after the two lines had inched closer and closer, Asofalinda and the other women shot out of line, raced to the campfire, grabbed sticks, and raced back to tap the men with the burning wood. Sparks flew and stung the men like angry bees.

Next everyone grabbed an ember and took it to a place where some of the younger men had prepared a moistened bed for the great honey fire. Instead of fire, however, the "honey fire" shot a dense cloud of smoke billowing up to the sky. While the men blew their honey whistles the women clapped and sang the magic song that along with the grey smoke would entice the bees back to make delicious, sticky, golden honey – the all-time favorite food of the Mbuti (Turnbull, 1968: 276–77).

Entertainment among the Ik (after generations of starvation)

Giriko's 10-year-old son Lokol suffered from a painful intestinal blockage. After a while, the boy couldn't eat or drink, and even lost the ability to vomit. Since it was too painful to sit up or lie down, he spent most of his time, even at night, balancing himself on his hands and knees, with his bloated stomach hanging to and resting on the ground.

Giriko considered all of this amusing, and used to call in the neighbors to get a look at Lokol and his distended belly. "It was a favorite topic for jokes," remarked anthropologist Colin Turnbull, who had tried without success to get the father to build a litter to carry the son to the hospital in Kaabong.

Turnbull brought food for Lokol, but several times had to physically restrain the boy's father from eating it himself (even though at that point, the father was not hungry). Lokol got better for a while, and his father again ushered in the neighbors – this time to watch his son defecate. Around this time Lokol seemed to lose interest in living. He died a short while later (Turnbull, 1972: 218–19).

Turnbull notes that the Ik lost interest in everything but food. Other than eating, the only thing that brought them pleasure was seeing others suffer. He watched mothers laugh with delight when their children were hurt or carried off by leopards. To the Ik, sexual intercourse was "a chore," the equivalent of a pleasurable bowel movement. One afternoon Turnbull watched two Ik on a hill mutually masturbating, all the while keeping a close eye out for any food that might pass by below.

Entertainment among Americans

In 2009, blue-eyed, 5'10'' Andrew Lohse from the sleepy little town of Branchburg, New Jersey, stunned Dartmouth College by spilling the beans to the world about the fraternity hazing that goes on at that ivy-league school. Among other indignities, frat wannabes suffered odiferous "baptisms" in a kiddie pool filled with feces, urine, semen and vomit.

Some of the Best and Brightest in American business and politics are born out of this baptism by fire on Dartmouth's

Hanover, New Hampshire, campus, including Jeffery Immelt, the CEO of GE, Morgan-Stanley senior adviser R. Bradford Evans, billionaire oilman Trevor Rees-Jones, venture capitalist William W. Helman IV, and former Secretary of the Treasury Hank Paulson. One of the first things Dartmouth boys learn is never to breathe a word about the torture that's the ticket to getting into this all-male, lucky-money club.

After breaking that sacred trust, Lohse became a Dartmouth pariah.

Other Dartmouth *rites de passage* involve ritual vomiting on frat members; forcing members to drink enough alcohol to kill them (and at other schools many a pledge have indeed died from alcohol poisoning, or water poisoning – the result of being forced to drink gallons in short time periods).

Sometimes pledges are allowed to stick their fingers down their throats to induce vomiting, which relieves the pain – this is called "pulling the trigger." Otherwise they must wait for a "higher" brother to perform the job for them.

Other forms of humiliation: being forced to eat "vomelets" – omelets made of vomit – being force-fed vinegar until one vomits blood, and being forced to drink beer poured over other men's anuses.

By the time Andrew Lohse finished his pledge term, he'd vomited so often that most of the enamel on his teeth had worn away.

As one of Lohse's SAE brothers puts it: "Having a 3.7 [grade-point average] and being the president of a hard-guy frat is far more valuable than having a 4.0 and being independent when it comes to going to a place like Goldman Sachs. And that corporate milieu mirrors the fraternity culture" (Reitman, 2012).

According to Hank Nuwer, professor at Indiana's Franklin College and author of four books on hazing, between 1970 and 2012 a full 104 American students died from hazing (Winerip, 2012).

Physical and mental abuse of children, the elderly, spouses, women, prostitutes, people of color and others could also be seen as a form of entertainment common in all state societies.

Violence (or the Lack of It)

Nonviolence among the Semai

The Semai of the Malay Peninsula are reputably one of the world's least violent societies. When speaking in Malay, a language foreign to them, the Semai often use the same word for "hit" as for "kill." To the Semai, hitting and killing are the same, the first as unthinkable as the second (Dentan, 1979: 58).

Astonishingly, when east Semai children play "hitting" games, no one is ever physically touched, and when they wrestle, no one is knocked to the ground. More than once anthropologist Robert Knox Dentan saw Semai children, both girls and boys, "flailing away" at each other with long sticks, all the while striking ferociously aggressive postures. However, their sticks would always stop abruptly, an inch or so away from their opponent's body.

Likewise, with wrestling: children aged two to ten wrestle their opponents within an inch or so of the ground, but never pin them, or even let their bodies touch ground. Dentan mused that these games were excellent training wheels, helping children learn how to live in their nonviolent society (Dentan, 1979: 59).

Child abuse, elder abuse, rape and war are unknown among the Semai.

Violence among the Ik (after generations of starvation)

When Atum was three his parents turned him out of the house, a round stick-built building under a thatched roof located inside their walled compound. (Atum's fate wasn't unusal – all Ik children are bounced out of their homes around the age of three.) It was no fun finding food on his own, or a warm place to sleep out of the rain. Sometimes Atum curled up on the ground under his parents' granary (a short silo raised on stick legs – which never had grain or any other food in it), or in a corner between the house and the compound wall.

Since all Ik parents locked out their three-year-olds, these babies stuck together in a tight-knit group of half a dozen to a dozen, for mutual protection and food-finding. Actually, three-year-olds joined the Ik "junior group," which included children from three to seven. At age eight, Atum would graduate into the senior group, aged eight to twelve. And at thirteen, he'd be an adult, forced out of all groups, and on his own.

Like all three-year-olds, Atum feared not only lions and leopards, but the members of his own group, who would have no qualms about beating him, grabbing whatever figs, berries or edible bark he'd uncovered, and gobbling them on the spot. So even after joining the junior group, Atum formed an alliance with Bila, also three, so that when Lokwam (age five), tried to manhandle either of them, they could fend him off.

When Atum turned seven, he was the strongest and became group leader. He told the group which *oror* (wooded mountain ravine) to scour for food. But if they scrambled down into a ravine and found a fig tree or ripe berries, and the senior band found them, the seniors would take over, lashing out at the smaller children with fists, sticks and stones until they ran away.

When he was old enough, the junior group turned on Atum, beating him and forcing him into the senior group. Atum's "friend" at the time, Lokelea, led the charge and became the junior group's new leader (just as Atum had turned against his "friend," the previous leader, when Atum himself had wanted to become chief of the group). Once in the senior group, Atum's status plummeted instantly from "oldest and strongest," to "weakest and most useless."

Violence among the Americans (football)

16-year-old Tom Cutinella, a tall, round-faced teen with a widow's peak and black hair skinned off in a buzz cut, slammed out of his Long Island, New York, home and raced toward the yellow school bus. Its motor rumbled as the driver sat patiently waiting for the six-foot, 185-pound football player to climb on board. But Cutinella skidded to a stop short of the bus, turned, and raced back to his house, shouting, "Dad! My jersey!"

Seconds later Frank Cutinella burst out of the house and threw the No. 54 football jersey at his son, who caught it mid-air.

"I love you, Dad!" Tom shouted, and started again for the idling bus. Halfway there, however, he skidded again to a stop, turning back toward his father.

"Tell Mom I love her!"

Those were the final words Frank Cutinella ever heard from his son. It was September, start of a new football season, and that night Tom was linebacker in a game pitting his school, Shoreham-Wading River, against John Glenn High. During the third quarter, Tom rammed his helmet into a Glenn player, trying to stop the guy from gaining ground. The crowd roared. Tom slowly climbed to his feet and wobbled toward the cheering. A few feet from the sideline, he collapsed.

On the way to Long Island's Huntington Hospital, emergency med techs inside the wailing ambulance worked feverishly on Tom. At the hospital surgeons operated on him for brain injury. When the surgery failed, Tom died.

"He always said 'I love you' to his family before going to school each morning," Frank Cutinella told newspaper reporters.

That season, sixteen-year-old Tom Cutinella was the third American high schooler in five days to die on the playing field from football injuries (Associated Press, 2014). Ken Belsen, writing in 2014 for *The New York Times* noted that "The National Football League, which for years disputed evidence that its players had a high rate of severe brain damage, has stated in federal court documents it expects nearly a third of retired players to develop long-term cognitive problems..."

Children

Children among the Utku Inuit

Of his four children, explained Inuttiaq from his home in the central Canadian Arctic, he loved his oldest and youngest "too much." Loving Saarak and Kamik too much meant when he was away on hunting or trading trips across the tundra he couldn't sleep nights for missing them, and when Kamik was away at school he felt "uncomfortable." "People don't like to feel uncomfortable," he observed. "If one doesn't love too much, it is good."

Inuit parents are notorious for their devotion to and indulgence of their children. Jean Briggs, who lived for 17 months with the Utku Inuit from 1963 to 1965, northwest of Hudson Bay at the frosty mouth of the Back River, says small children are "snuffed, cuddled, cooed at, talked to, and played with endlessly, the men as demonstrative as the women" (Briggs, 1995: 70).

This describes perfectly Inuttiaq with his baby daughter Saarak. When her father was away Saarak was cranky, and when he came home, she bounced with excitement. He'd shake her hand, hold her on his lap, and at night cuddle her beside him, cooing tenderly to her while she slept.

When his daughter Kamik went away to college, Inuttiaq was sad. In April he began talking about her return for the summer. He bought her a new sleeping bag and flannel cloth for a new parka. For her homecoming, he saved one of the eight caribou he had killed the previous August.

But come May, the government plane failed to touch down at Back River. Inuttiaq thought maybe Kamik had been dropped off at the wrong place, and drove his dogsled three days through slushy spring snow to Umanak Island, about halfway down

Chantrey Inlet, to look for her. Returning home alone he was despondent, and lay in his usual spot in the tent smoking his pipe, drinking tea, and looking at no one.

But when Kamik's plane finally dropped down onto the ice of the Back River that same afternoon, Inuutiaq was first out of the tent. Along with Kamik's family, Jean Briggs too sloshed through the knee-deep spring snow to reach Kamik's plane, which was now bouncing along the river ice to a stop.

Inuit adults are shy with each other, and so it was between Kamik and her family when she climbed off the plane. But Inuttiaq grabbed his daughter's duffel bag and listened intently as she told stories about the strange ways of the whites: loud and angry all the time, hitting their children, letting babies cry, kissing adults, and keeping dogs and cats as pets (Briggs, 1995: 69–74).

Children among the Ik (after decades of group-wide starvation)

British anthropologist Colin Turnbull had taken to feeding Adupa, a young Ik girl whose family lived in the compound next to his. Like all Ik children, Adupa was locked out of her house at age three. After they're evicted, kids band together in age-grade groups for protection. For some reason, however, even her age group rejected Adupa, who was wasting away. The other children loved to drop food in her path, watch her pick it up and move it toward her mouth. At precisely this point, her mates would swoop in, yank away the food, and "beat her savagely over the head."

So Adupa had no choice but to try to win her way into her parents' hearts. She'd lovingly bring them food scrounged from Turnbull knew not where – fruit peels, skins, bits of bone, half-eaten berries. But her parents only snatched the food and slammed the door in her face. Finally, one day the couple opened their house to Adupa and then left, shutting the door to their compound tightly.

Adupa's parents stayed away for days. Too weak to break out of the compound, Adupa died there, and when her parents returned, her body was badly decomposed. Her parents carried it, "as one does the riper garbage," far from the house, flinging it into a field. They piled rocks on it, so vultures and hyenas would not drag Adupa's body around the neighborhood and offend the neighbors.

Children among Americans

On August 1, 2014, Rodney Shoeman responded to a 911 call in Harrisburg, PA. As soon as he climbed out of his patrol car at the home of Jarrod Tutko, Sr., he smelled "a strong odor of decomposition." Inside the house the odor was almost unbearable. Jarrod Jr.'s mother, Kimberly Tutko, who was separated from his father, couldn't understand why there was such a stench in her husband's house. She thought it was dead mice, and she'd tried to eliminate the smell with mothballs and bleach (Associated Press, 2014).

In actual fact, the stench was coming from the dead body of Jarrod Jr. Mr. Tutko had locked the boy in a third-floor bedroom with no food, furniture, lights, or toilet. The boy had finally died of starvation. On the day of his death, nine-year-old Jarrod, Jr., weighed 16 pounds. In the middle of Jarrod's room officer Shoeman found a feces-smeared stuffed rabbit and blanket – the boy's bed. The room's light switch and doorknob were smeared with feces. In fact, the entire room was covered with a thick layer of body waste, and flies swarmed everywhere. The room's bolted-down TV was tuned to the Disney channel. "I can only imagine what it was like on a hot summer day in that room," District Attorney Ed Marsico said.

Jarrod's corpse showed signs of severe dental decay. A dentist reported that at time of death the boy would have been in extreme pain. When Jarrod was born, Mr. and Mrs. Tutko were unable to take him home immediately, because they were being investigated for abuse of Jarrod's sister.

In 2011, the 50 US states reported 676,569 victims of child abuse and neglect. In the same year, allegations of abuse and neglect were reported for 6.2 million children (Jackson, 2014; Scolforo, 2014). "The data collection system on child deaths is so flawed that no one can even say with accuracy how many children overall die from abuse or neglect every year," say Holbrook Mohr and Garance Burke, writing for the Associated Press in December 2014. "Child abuse is found at all social levels, from paupers to royalty," say Murray Straus and Christine Smith in *Physical Violence in Families*.

Sharing Vs Hoarding

Sharing among the Semai

With his poison darts and eight-foot blowpipe (two hollow bamboo poles hooked together), Bah Chong ventured out one sultry day into the Malaysian rain forest to hunt. After trekking for four days along narrow, steamy jungle paths, fighting biting insects and slippery clay slopes, he'd still had no luck.

Finally, on the morning of the fifth day, he spied a large pig. Quickly he shoved a dart into the far end of his blowpipe, its tip dabbed with a sticky poison made from toadskin, snake venom, *Strychnos*-vine juice, and sap from the upas tree. After stuffing a bit of tree cotton in to keep the dart in place, Bah raised the weapon to his lips, blew, and scored a direct hit on the pig's left side. Squealing, the animal scrambled away through thick jungle underbrush.

After following the wounded animal through a deep-green sea of brush, Bah shot a few more poison darts, and the pig collapsed and died. Sweating in the sticky heat, Bah lugged the pig home, and upon reaching his village dropped it to the ground. Soon the entire village was swarming around the carcass. Bah stood aside as two other men, Roi and Rambutan, began to carve the dead animal, slicing through its skin and hot, red entrails. They divided the animal into bundles, all equal in weight and contents, each designed to feed two adults (Semai children are forbidden to eat pork).

Roi and Rambutan were extremely careful to get exactly the same amount of meat, fat and innards into each bundle, which they wrapped in large leaves for villagers to carry home. No one thanked Bah for the meat; to do so would be rude, implying Bah was too stingy to share (Dentan, 1979: 14, 31, 48–49). To the Semai not to share when you have extra and obviously don't need it all, is "punan," i.e., taboo. Violence and the failure to share are one and the same, both equally shameful (Dentan, 1978: 134).

Hoarding among the Ik (after generations of starvation)

Although at one time they might have been a sharing people like the Semai, when anthropologist Colin Turnbull knew them the Ik had mastered the fine art of hoarding. One day Turnbull trekked with some of the men down the mountain trail into the town of Kasile, on a famine-relief expedition. These were the few Ik still strong enough to walk. Their ostensible mission: to bring food back to their sick and dying.

After collecting the food, the group began the long trek home. A few miles beyond Kasile, however, too soon for a rest stop, the group veered off the trail into the bushes. There they "gobble[d] and gorge[d] themselves until they were bloated and had to vomit." A few postponed gorging until a bit further down the trail, where they could eat at a more leisurely pace.

One man only, Kauar, turned his back on the others and stared into the distance while they ate. He was taking food back to his sick wife and child. The others jeered at him for carrying the load on his head when he could be carrying it in his stomach (Turnbull, 1972: 282 – 83).

In the village, when people stumbled onto food, they gobbled it immediately. Often, they ate running, so no one could dig the food out of their mouths before they swallowed (Turnbull, 1972: 262). This was such "normal" behavior, that after a while Turnbull failed even to notice it.

Once again remember: Ik society was affected physically and mentally by generations of starvation. Starving people do strange things, including almost anything at all if it means they can eat. And when children grow up seeing only bizarre behavior everywhere, this is the behavior they exhibit as adults, and pass on to their children, and their children's children. And so on...

Hoarding among Americans

Psychologist Randy Frost wants to help his patient Debra recover from her hoarding obsession. He begins with an easy step: he sends her a postcard empty except for her name, address and a stamp which she is to remove from her mailbox and throw away.

Debra, however, is unable to part with the card. "I haven't had enough time with it," she wails to Randy, after lovingly describing the card's stamp and postmark. Eventually she manages to pitch the card. She tells Randy she can vividly recall the card's exact location in her trash. Later she also admits that after pitching the card she filled several pages of notes about it, recording everything she could remember: postmark, picture on the stamp, size of the stamp, typeface, etc. She plans to save these notes (Kramer, 2010).

If you live in North America you might have watched one or more episodes of the long-running, highly popular reality-television series "Hoarders" (or one of its various spinoffs: "Hoarders: Family Secrets," "Hoarders: Then and Now," or "Hoarders Overload"). The series began in 2009 and is still running.

The Elderly

The Elderly among the !Kung (aka San, Bushmen, Juwasi and Zhu/oasi)

Among the !Kung of southern Africa the elders know things young people don't: the details of past scandals, for example, where to find food in lean years, old folktales, who's related to whom, and when the first anthropologists came. And, if something strange happens, older people have seen it all, and they can tell you how to respond. Their opinions matter, they are asked for advice, and they are willingly shown affection (Shostak, 1983: 324). The oldest member of the family in the area longest, owns all the food and water (this person, however, rarely denies that food or water to anyone).

The elderly provide one of the main sources of !Kung entertainment: storytelling. A storyteller might spin tales about the times when animals were people and could talk, or about the people with no knees, called the "Knee Knee None" (aka "The People Who Eat the Sun"). Or about the fight between the hare and the moon: the hare insisted that at death we are gone forever, but the moon begged to differ, offering itself as a prime example: didn't the moon, once a month, die, and return a few days later (Marshall, 2000)?

A good !Kung storyteller pulls out a deep voice for the moon, and a high, scratchy one for the hare. She makes the sound of the wind whistling through the bushes, and of the hare scratching up sand. When the moon is sad, the storyteller might hunch her shoulders, or turn down her mouth, and when the hare is happy, she might throw her arms into the air. In a way, it's better than moving-picture shows, since you have a flesh-and-blood actor sitting where you can almost feel her breath on your neck, and the warmth from her body radiating over to yours (Shostak, 1983: 324–25).

The Elderly among the Ik (after generations of starvation)

If you're elderly, the Ik are not the people you want to live with. After suffering starvation conditions for generations, the Ik turned into what I call a "starvation culture" – one most Western observers would probably call psychotic. Colin Turnbull, the anthropologist who tried to feed them but failed, describes Ik elders as "semi-animate bags of skin and bone... [with] the blotchy look of a corpse that has been smoked" (Turnbull, 1972:222–23). Too weak to walk, elders crawled. "Crawling" meant sitting on your backside, dropping your knuckles to the ground between your legs, and raising yourself a hair off the ground – just enough to swing yourself forward an inch or two "like a pendulum." This process is repeated until you reach your destination.

Mostly, the elderly wanted to get near another old person, after which they would sit silently. Turnbull said the elderly "moved like slugs, in danger of being trampled underfoot but seemingly unaware of it, concentrating only on covering the next few feet of ground ahead of them" (Turnbull, 1972: 225).

One day Turnbull witnessed the following. A group of young hunters strolled into the village empty-handed from the hunt. Although they'd been attacked by a buffalo and lost half a spear fighting, they were laughing and shouting. In the village the first thing the hunters did was order children to bring them water. These were older children soon to move into adulthood, but they ran off immediately to the village watering hole. Instead of fetching water, however, the youngsters began splashing and playing in the muddy pond. Nearby a few skeletal elderly were crawling along on knuckles and bottoms. When the children tired of their water games, they turned to "play with" the elders.

One girl picked a white flower, tied it to a vine, and swung it around her head as she danced around Ngorok, one of the elders. At times she stood in front of Ngorok, blocking his progress whichever way he turned. Lokwam stood watching. Lokwam was an especially handsome boy, and this day he'd tied broad bands of grass tightly around his calves, arms, and forehead, making him more handsome than ever. At some point, Lokwam got into the game. Instead of merely blocking Ngorok's progress, however, Lokwam took great delight in lightly pushing him and the other elders, so that they "teetered and then toppled" off their bottoms. "It was a time of fun and laughter for all," said Turnbull, facetiously (Turnbull, 1972: 222–24).

The Elderly among Americans

Seattle, Washington, November, 2012:

Leaving a trail of blood through his house and across his lawn, paramedics carried 86-year-old Kyle Shaw down his stairs in a chair, and out to the ambulance. The stairs were the worst: at each step the man screamed in pain. When the medics found Kyle, he wore only a T-shirt and a pair of bloodied, feces-covered socks that had grown into his feet. Kyle died soon after reaching the Swedish Medical Center, where physicians found him caked with filth and suffering from multiple life-threatening ailments, including rotting feet.

Kyle had substantial savings – far and away enough to purchase a place in a good nursing home for himself and his wife. But his 50-something sons Keith and Ken wanted the money. So they moved in with their parents, living rent-free while they "cared for" the elderly couple. When a nurse suggested the two men move their mother into a nursing home, Keith objected. "Why should we clean out the accounts?" he said. "I don't have any retirement and Ken's never worked… If we spend all the money on nursing homes (Ken) will end up homeless, living under the viaduct" (Pulkkinen, 2012).

According to the National Center on Elder Abuse, Administration on Aging, Health and Human Services, "[T] he vast majority of abusers [of American elderly are] family members... most often adult children, spouses, partners, and others."

The above suggests that Americans look more like starving people than like the world's remaining healthy groups. Although there's no room here to include similar comparisons using the UK, Canada, Australia, Japan, or other state societies, such comparisons would show the same: state societies in general resemble starving people far more than they do healthy human groups. How did this happen? How did things plummet into this sorry state of affairs? This is the subject of the next chapter, and of most of the rest of the book.

Chapter 4

Not Born to Be Bad

Over the centuries we've tried so hard to scrub away our warts. But for all our efforts, we've succeeded about as well as we have in locating the Loch Ness Monster. You'd almost think we humans, as the song goes, are "born to be bad":

> Now on the night I arrived
> My daddy said "Sake's Alive!"
> It's the meanest one that we've had yet
> Teethed on tin and weaned on gin
> I was nobody's teacher's pet
> Born, born to be bad
> I was born
> Born to be bad. (1988, George Thorogood and the Destroyers)

Around 500 BCE the ancient Greeks created democracies – but lost them after only a few centuries. The Romans lost their republic in 44 BCE with the assassination of Julius Caesar by the Roman Senate. By the nineteenth century slavery was abolished throughout much of the world – but social inequality still remains to sting us even today in societies across the globe.

In the US, Americans have knocked themselves out to eliminate poverty (think Lyndon Johnson's 1960s "War on Poverty," for example). But instead of fading away, the number of poor Americans has stubbornly mushroomed over the past forty years. What's more, there's no sign on the horizon that rates of violence, child abuse, elder abuse, spousal abuse, drug use or general crime rates are falling either. Most of the world now agrees that war is not a noble pursuit, and many even see it primarily as a game waged by the rich on the backs of the poor. And since the advent of nuclear weapons, almost all of us agree that war is a game no longer safe to play. Nevertheless, war has not flapped away over the horizon the way we wish it would. With the end of the Cold War in 1991 many Westerners actually thought they'd seen the end of warfare, but by 1994 – only three years later – the US became mired down in the Bosnian War, in 1998 the Kosovo War, in 2001 the war in Afghanistan, in 2003 in Iraq and in 2011 the conflict in Syria.

In other words, no matter how hard we try we can't seem to rid ourselves of the swarm of ills plaguing our "state" societies. But it's not because we were "born bad." On the contrary, it's because we don't understand the underlying causes of these ills. You might be able to kick a problem to the curb temporarily, but then that pesky underlying cause kicks in once more, giving birth to the problem all over again.

Not Born to Do War

So, state societies have ugly social issues we can't seem to wash out of our collective hair. In general, social scientists tag one of two causes for human behavior: nature or nurture, biology or upbringing. Take war, for example. Do humans fight because we're born violent, or because we learn to fight from the adults around us? Actually, there's a war going on about war, with one side – sometimes called "the Hawks" – insisting war is baked into our genes, and the other side, "the Doves" insisting it is not, that it is learned behavior – and can be unlearned – or not learned in the first place.

A major heavyweight champion on the side of the Doves is one Douglas Fry, Director of Peace, Mediation and Conflict Research at Finland's Abo Akademi University, and a research scientist in anthropology at the University of Arizona. Mr. Fry says it's a myth that war is inevitable. War is not hardwired into our species, he says. Fry's the author of three books on war and peace, all three published by the prestigious Oxford University Press: *Beyond War*; *The Human Potential for Peace*; and *War, Peace and Human Nature*. The latter is a relatively recent collection of essays covering a wide range of topics, from the peacefulness of our primate cousin the bonobo, to how hard military leaders have to sweat to get soldiers over their natural aversion to killing human beings. The essay "Pinker's List: Exaggerating Prehistoric War Mortality" debunks the false notion that war was ubiquitous before around 4000 BCE. As a matter of fact, says the essay's author, "...war was absent in entire prehistoric regions and for millennia" at a time (Fry, 2013: 126).

Actually, anyone who knows anything about anthropology or culture studies knows the Doves are on the winning side here. Even now, after most of the world's indigenous societies have been crushed, creamed and obliterated, a handful of such societies remain alive and kicking, many of them almost completely nonviolent. A prime example: the Semai of Southeast Asia, population as of 2007: 43,500 (PeacefulSocieties.org).

The Semai live in the center of the Malay Peninsula, and are thought to be Malaysia's original inhabitants. These amazing people are so nonviolent that, as mentioned previously, when their children play games "hitting" each other with sticks, the sticks never actually touch anyone. Instead they stop abruptly an inch or so above a child's body. And when the Semai wrestle and "throw someone to the ground," nobody ever actually reaches the ground, but is held an inch or two above it. The Semai believe that hitting children could cause them to get sick and die. Needless to say, the Semai don't engage in warfare, and to escape it they will, if necessary, move their villages further into the forest. Nor are they violent toward each other or toward strangers.

Although the Semai come close to being totally nonviolent, they aren't born that way. As children the Semai are taught to fear anger, especially their own, and an anthropologist who asked a sample of Semai to complete the sentence "More than anything else I am afraid of _____," discovered that the respondents were more afraid of interpersonal conflict than of tigers, "malevolent spirits" or death *combined* (Fry, 2005: 74). Children are also taught the world is alive with danger, and that safety lies in being part of a close-knit, harmonious group. They're also taught that to keep another group member happy sometimes it's necessary to sacrifice one's own desires.

Never are Semai children pushed to do things they don't want to do, and except for an occasional mild pinch on the cheek or a light pat on the hand they're never punished. When children fight, they are plucked up by the nearest adult and carried away from play and into a house to cool off.

Of course like all other humans on planet Earth, the Semai occasionally get angry. But if two parties can't resolve their differences, they are gossiped about or shamed. Or one or both parties might temporarily move out of the village. If none of the above work, villagers gather in a meeting called a *bcaraa'* (PeacefulSocieties.org), in which both parties get to tell their story – for as long as they want. *Bcaraa'* often drag on for hours, until everyone is exhausted, at which time the village leader closes the meeting with a long speech about the importance of group harmony. The leader may or may not slap a small fine on one or both parties to the dispute.

The Semai are not the only nonviolent group left in the world. For several years the Anthropology Department at the University of Alabama at Birmingham has tended a webpage called "Peaceful Societies: Alternatives to Violence and War." This site includes a constantly updated encyclopedia of peaceful world societies, which, in addition to the Semai includes the Amish, Batek, Birhor, Buid, Chewong, Fipa, G/wi, Hutterites, Ifaluk, Inuit of Utkuhikhalik and Qipisa Communities, Ju/'hoansi, Kadar, Ladakhi, Lepchas, Malapandaram, Mbuti, Nubians, Paliyans, Piaroa, the Rural Thai, Tahitians, Tristan Islanders,

Yanadi, and the Zapotec of La Paz Village, Mexico.

Because several human groups don't do war, war cannot be a natural part of the human condition. But how about the other bad stuff – poverty, hierarchy, crime and such? Same thing. The other bad stuff can't be biologically-based either, because societies exist without such blights. As do countless other human societies, the Semai live without poverty, crime, inequality, rape, drug abuse, and so forth. Because they have no need for them, many societies don't even have police forces.

Warfare before 4000 BCE?

So, surprise, surprise: people free of warfare, out-of-control crime, social snobbery and the other blights encrusting our starvation-culture societies, do exist today in the world. But what about in the past? Turns out here too there's no good evidence that before around 4000 BCE humans were much bothered by war, poverty, snobs, or crime. "War sprang out of a warless world," says Rutgers University anthropologist R. Brian Ferguson, a veteran scholar of warfare who published his first tome on the topic in 1984 (Ferguson, 2013a: 229). Keith F. Otterbein, Professor Emeritus of Anthropology at the University at Buffalo (SUNYAB), says war began at two separate times in history. The first, he says, arose two million years ago "at the dawn of humankind." People who hunted and gathered "for a living" says Otterbein, sometimes fell into armed conflict with other hunters. But when agriculture began – around 10,000 BCE, give or take a few millennia, depending on where you are in the world – war dropped out of sight for a while. Otterbein sees little or no evidence of warfare during this long stretch of human history. He also thinks it would have been impossible for agriculture to get a toehold in places that engaged in much warfare.

According to Otterbein, war popped up around 4000 BCE – after hibernating for 6000 years – "among peaceful agricultural peoples, whose societies first achieved statehood and then proceeded to embark upon military conquests (Otterbein, 2004: 3)." Otterbein says the four "pristine" states, which he says arose in Mesopotamia, China, Mexico and Peru, were all followed by a resurgence of warfare. A pristine state is the first one to arise in any world area; as time marched on, each pristine state would spin off "offspring" states all around itself.

Otterbein, by the way, defines war as "...the activities of military organizations, groups of men – under the direction of leaders – who engage in armed combat" (Otterbein, 2004: 4). (I would have used the word "people" instead of "men," since at times throughout history women too have formed such military organizations.) Otterbein says the main war leader is the society's head honcho (later in his book we'll call this guy "Alpha"), and under the head honcho are lieutenants, who are always members of the aristocracy (in this book we'll call them members of "the elite"). At the very bottom of the whole shebang are the poor slobs who make up the bulk of the population, and who actually show their skin to the opposition's weaponry, for slicing and dicing. These poor souls are conscripts, society's underclass, and they usually "agree" to their soldier status only after being violently forced into it, in one way or another.

In 2013, archaeologists Haas and Piscitelli went even further than Otterbein, sashaying forth with good evidence that war was unknown "at the dawn of humankind." Haas and Piscitelli complain that Otterbein (and others) have extrapolated from modern nomadic hunter-gatherers back to prehistoric ones. But, they say, you can't judge prehistoric hunters by current ones, because for millennia the current ones have been treated like punching bags by the big state societies:

> Otterbein and followers, in turning to the historic ethnographic record to support their claims of the ubiquity of warfare in the prehistoric past, fail to consider how hunters and gatherers of

> the "ethnographic present" may be profoundly different from hunters and gatherers of the more distant archaeological past. How many of these [prehistoric] societies were surrounded... by existing states; pushed by the rippling effects of other refugees; armed by traders; provoked... by missionaries; cut off from traditional lands? (Haas and Piscitelli, 2013: 173–74)

Prehistorian James C. Scott agrees: it's impossible to "triangulate" from modern hunter-gatherers back to our prehistoric past, the way popular writers like Jared Diamond mistakenly do. The reason? Modern hunter-gatherers aren't "museum exhibits" – they've changed through the millennia just like the rest of us. Hunter-gatherers are not our "living ancestors," says Scott (2013). And much of that change has to do with the battering most of them have taken at the hands of state societies.

If Haas, Piscitelli and Scott are right – most experts now say they are – serious warfare did not begin until around 4000 BCE, when peaceful farming towns suddenly morphed into monstrous state societies, and soon after became addicted to wars of conquest. But why did this happen? What would have turned small-scale peaceful peoples – perhaps much like the Semai – into vicious, large-scale monsters, almost overnight?

Chapter 5

Some of Us Act Like Starving People

The number of traits state societies share with long-starving people is truly eye-opening. While starving, Ik individuals spent much time ripping things away from their family members and neighbors, Americans do too – through armed robbery, murder, rape, incest, slavery and warfare. After Ik society fell apart, Ik brothers stole from sisters, parents pilfered from children, and children snatched food directly out of the mouths of the elderly. And instead of sharing food even with family members, the strongest Ik literally ate it all – or as much as they could until vomiting.

Like the Ik, Americans too have serious problems with food. One in three Americans is obese, and increasingly academics are labeling obesity an American epidemic. Not one of the 50 US states can claim an obesity rate under 20%, and obesity is a cause of major health problems including Type II diabetes, cardiovascular disease and cancer (Emmett and Chandra, 2015: 92). And obesity isn't just an American problem. In Canada, 18.3% of adults are obese – up from 6.1% in 1985 (Jessri, Wolfinger, Lou and L'Abbe, 2017: 669). What's more, "recent evidence points to levels of obesity rising among populations throughout Europe, Southeast Asia, and the third world, so that the epidemic has taken on a global dimension" (Speakman, 2007).

But in addition to obesity, anorexia, bulimia and binge eating can be added to the list of American food-related demons. People with binge eating disorder (BED) tend to gobble down large quantities of food in short order, and are often either overweight or obese. In contrast, bulemics binge eat but follow their bingeing with purging, or vomiting, which lets them avoid obesity. Instead of binge eating, anorexics starve themselves, and are underweight; technically anorexics have lost at least 15% of their ideal body weight. In other words, just as the Ik have an overwhelming and sometimes deadly preoccupation with food, so do many Americans.

Like the Ik too, Americans enjoy watching others suffer. Whether it's football, professional wrestling, dog fighting, cock fighting, or violent films, TV and music, many of us pay to gawk at the suffering of others. Although the Ik had no organized sports or electronic media, they nevertheless managed to invent ways to place suffering people in the limelight. This included knocking over the elderly in public (and laughing as they fell), and inviting neighbors in to watch children suffer acute illness.

Like the Ik, Americans and those in other state societies hoard. Instead of food, however, we hoard money and things. In fact some of us even suffer from hoarding disorder, or "household hoarding," our homes crisscrossed by narrow paths winding through shoulder-high stacks of papers, mail, books, clothing, cardboard boxes, plastic bags, magazines, and other paraphernalia. Since their sinks, showers and beds are piled high with things, severe hoarders even have trouble washing dishes, showering and sleeping.

Other hoarders obsessively build their bank accounts. Why would a billionaire fight tooth and nail to amass a second or third billion? What's the point? And yet this is exactly how many of us hustle through our days: by working to stockpile more money than anyone could shell out in 100 lifetimes.

For the Ik, nothing snagged their attention like food. Even their games focused on food (Turnbull, 1972: 144). Nothing could compete with food, not even sexuality. Sex was not the pleasurable and bonding experience it is among healthy people, but only "a necessary chore" (Turnbull, 1972: 253), with sexual intercourse being unassociated with the love and respect healthy partners feel for one another. For the Ik, sex was a perfunctory act sometimes even performed in public – so participants could keep an eye out for food that might pass by during the sex act. Colin Turnbull, the anthropologist who lived among the Ik, used the term "mutual masturbation" to label the Ik attitude toward sex (Turnbull, 1972: 254).

For many Americans too sexuality seems to be negative and unhealthy. For example, sex is often the butt of jokes – as if sexuality at its core is a joke. What's more, much of our humor centers on the scatological, and terms for sex equate sexuality with anger, disgust, mental illness and failure ("fuck you," "she's a boob," "he's a dick," "she's a cunt," "he's fucked up," "I fucked up," "I was fucked over," "get the fuck out of here," and so forth). And according to some estimates as many as half of American women, at some point in their lives, will be raped or incested. Meanwhile, prostitution cheapens all state societies, but unlike Ik women, who sold their bodies for food, state-society women are more likely to sell theirs for money.

Another result of the Ik's long-term lack of food and nutrition was the bleeding away of family ties. When Colin Turnbull lived among the Ik, family ties had faded away to nothing, blood relatives rarely interacting with one another (Turnbull, 1972: 114). For example, men typically abandoned their children, and mothers abused children until, at age three, offspring were unceremoniously tossed out of the house. Brothers stole from sisters, and, as mentioned earlier, one child who begged her parents once too often for food was shut up in the house and left to die (Turnbull, 1972: 132). Turnbull even witnessed a man completely ignoring his father as the older man dragged himself along the ground, too weak from hunger even to crawl (Turnbull, 1972: 225).

Although American family ties are meatier than the Ik's, when viewed alongside those of the Semai or !Kung, they appear somewhat pathetic. Like Ik fathers, many American fathers too abandon their families, becoming "deadbeat dads," or virtually disappearing to work in different US states, or to work multiple jobs, or to sail off to war in foreign lands. In America, divorce, incest and child abuse are rampant, along with elder and spouse abuse. What's more, extended families are a thing of the past, with the individual, and especially the "rugged individual" the real hero. For many Americans it's a "me generation," a "my way or the highway" country, riddled with anxiety, anomie, panic attacks and depression. In a recent American TV commercial, a group of young males are featured singing a loud, lusty, chorus of "I want it all, and I want it NOW!"

Among the Ik not only family ties but social ties too had grown as thin and diluted as a weak cup of watery tea. There were, of course, good reasons for this. Unless people ate alone or while running, they risked having food literally snatched straight out of their mouths. And if it meant increased food or power, childhood friends became enemies overnight. Youngsters constantly bullied each other, prompting Ik children to form age-grade gangs for protection against not only wild animals and starvation, but against each other as well.

Like the Ik, Americans too often eat alone, either at home, or in restaurants surrounded by strangers. Many families seldom eat together as a family. As do Ik children, many American kids too form gangs for mutual protection, while bullying, including cyber bullying, has exploded into a national epidemic.

Politically, the Ik were as democratic as Kim Jung Un's North Korea. Among them, the physically strong ran the show according to their own desires, taking every opportunity to bully the weak. Individual Ik were often forced to fend for themselves with no help from others. In contrast individuals in many indigenous societies crank out important decisions together, as a group, usually on a consensual basis – everyone must agree on where the new council house will be built, for example, before construction begins, and leaders are chosen based on the task, whether it's caribou hunting, planting rice, or resolving a neighborhood squabble.

When it comes to political systems America lies somewhere between the Ik and the happier indigenous groups discussed at the beginning of this book. Typically, American workplaces shake out as totally authoritarian: supervisors behave like dictators, customers behave like dictators, and like rats in a trap, the average worker is caught in between the two. Although in the past, American labor unions insured workers at least a voice in the workplace, unions today have become scarce as icicles on a hot day in July.

Like its job sites, America's schools too are anti-democratic. The "No Child Left Behind Act" and its successor, "The Every Child Succeeds Act," strip teachers of much of their decision-making power. And with school boards perched on the apex of the power pyramid, school superintendents under them, principals under superintendents, and teachers flattened out under principals, students flounder at the very bottom of the pyramid, rarely sharing in the educational decision-making process. In contrast, Semai children freely explore and learn from their environment, and for Semai adults to force children to do anything is taboo.

Some of the best of America's political system was borrowed from its original indigenous people, the "First Americans." For centuries before the first shots were fired at Lexington and Concord in 1775, the Iroquois Nation had nurtured a federalist system of government. In 1775 there were no democracies in Europe for the American colonists to copy. But more than one Founding Father was intimately acquainted with the Iroquois. For instance, during his tenure as Pennsylvania's official printer, Benjamin Franklin published Indian treaties, Indian speeches, and Indian council-meeting records, and Native Americans fascinated him so much that he conducted his own research into their cultures. As early as 1754 Franklin advised the colonies to use the League of the Iroquois as their model for uniting together as one political entity:

> Benjamin Franklin first became acquainted with the operation of Indian political organization in his capacity as official printer for the colony of Pennsylvania... Because of his expertise and interest in Indian matters... Pennsylvania offered him his first diplomatic assignment as their Indian commissioner. He held this post during the 1750s, and became intimately familiar with the intricacies of Indian political culture and in particular with the League of the Iroquois. After this taste of Indian diplomacy, Franklin became a lifelong champion of the Indian political structure and advocated its use by the Americans. (Weatherford, 1988: 136)

The League of the Iroquois consisted of five nations: the Mohawk, Onondaga, Seneca, Oneida and Cayuga, each of which had a national council of "sachems," elected by Iroquois villages. Each Iroquoian national council sent its sachems to the League's grand council, which met at least every five years, and if necessary more often. The grand council made policy affecting the entire League: about war and peace, for example, and treaties, and ambassadorships.

With a few tweaks, the Iroquois political system was adopted by the American colonists after the colonists won their freedom from Great Britain. One tweak was the American Presidency. The indigenous Iroquois had no need of a single, grand leader, while the starvation-culture colonists were incapable of abandoning the idea of a Great-Father figure who could magically solve all problems. Another: the colonists slammed the door on female participation in government. In contrast, women played central roles in the government of the healthy, indigenous Iroquois.

On the other hand, the Colonists adopted certain Iroquois peculiarities verbatim, and these still distinguish American from European politics. For example, while Britain's Parliament is known for its noisy, boisterous cacophony, the Colonists adopted the Iroquois rule that in Congress only one person may speak at a time. Also like the Iroquois, Americans are never to address Congressional members by personal name, but as "Madam Speaker," "the Representative from Rhode Island," or "the Senator from California" (Weatherford, 1988: 136–4).

Yes, the Founding Fathers were well-read in the ancient Greek and Roman democracies and used aspects of these political systems too, in order to create their new United States. But Greece and Rome languished far in the past, reachable only by the printed word. The League of the Iroquois on the other hand, was a living, breathing democratic system existing right under the Fathers' noses, one they could study first hand.

Now that I've convinced you that Americans (and all other state societies) are half Ik, I want to be clear: you can't blame yourself – or anyone else – for this bad news. We certainly can't blame ourselves, since we were brainwashed as young, pliable humans into Ik-style behavior. But we can't blame our ancestors either, any more than we can blame a schizophrenic for hearing voices coming out of the toaster oven. Blaming ourselves is not only unfair, it makes us feel like jumping off the nearest cliff.

One of my favorite wise men, Jiddu Krishnamurti, says it's unproductive to think that anything you do is bad. Nothing you do, he says, is good *or* bad – it just is. And your job is to look at this behavior, nothing else. When I manage to talk myself into believing nothing I do is good or bad, something amazing happens: an overwhelming wave of relief washes over me, and I spin into a new force field vis-à-vis behavior I might otherwise feel guilt, shame or confusion over. And this absence of guilt or shame makes it easier for me to see the causes and poisonous results of my behavior – which frees me up to change it.

Humans Aren't Born Knowing How to Build Their Nests

Until now we've mostly painted a picture of starvation behavior by comparing various humans who suffer from it with those who don't. From here on out, however, we'll deal with where this ugly behavior came from, and how it managed to skewer the world. Since the Semai, !Kung, Mbuti, Inuit and others aren't violent, greedy and lonely, violence, greediness and loneliness can't be things we're born with. So how *did* Americans and others get stuck with them?

The answer lies in the past, in something I call "starvation culture." What is culture? Not what you get by spending time with Bach, Brahms, Sartre, Picasso or Miss Manners. I'm not talking here about that kind of culture. The kind I am talking about is defined as the way of life of any human group. The world contains thousands of different cultures, each with its own special, unique set of rules for living: British culture, French culture, Southeast Asian culture, Brazilian culture, and so on. As we'll see below, these rules are learned, shared by everyone in your group, coordinated into one big, happy whole, and are inherited by you from the people who came before you.

The Rules Are Learned

Your culture doesn't come from your genes, your biology or your body chemistry, it all comes from learning. You learn your culture from your parents, school teachers, the media, and all the adults around you. You were not born knowing the rules of your culture. You had to soak them up as you grew.

The Rules Are Shared

The rules for living that make up your group's culture are more or less shared by everyone in your group. Humans who fail to follow the rules of their group almost always get in trouble – they're poked fun of, shunned, imprisoned, or – if the rules they break are serious enough, even executed. Some people who fail to abide by certain kinds of their group's rules are forced out of the group, or locked away in mental institutions.

The Rules Are Coordinated

A culture's rules are all coordinated. They all mesh together like the parts of a truck mesh together. If truck parts don't mesh, the truck won't work, and if the rules of a culture don't mesh, the culture won't work either – not well at least. Another metaphor: a culture's rules for living all fit together like the gears in a smoothly-running clock. The result? Everyone's ideas, tastes, predilections, beliefs, behaviors, mannerisms and even something as concrete as their clothing – all these things more or less fit together one with the other, seamlessly, without a hitch in the picture as a whole.

The Rules Are Inherited

Whether you realize it or not, you teach all these coordinated rules to your children. And they pass them on to their children. And so on, down through the ages, down through time. Like the Olympic torch, culture is passed from one generation to the next, ad infinitum – or if and when your culture dies. You inherit your culture, in other words, from those who came before you.

Of course, some of the rules of your culture will change a bit as they slide through time, but not many will, and none will change all that much. Even though the British and the French live right next door to one another, their cultures are as different as peacocks from hummingbirds. This has nothing to do with genes or biology. It's all due to the fact that, from the time they're born, British and French people each learn different sets of rules for how to behave. Just one example: even though they've been next-door neighbors for millennia, the French turn out mouth-watering cuisine and awesome art, while the British do neither (not as well anyway). On the other hand, the French have never turned out a William Shakespeare.

If you'd strip the human race of culture, our entire species would go belly-up in a hurry. I'd give us a year, tops. While animals burst right out of the womb knowing much of what they need to know to survive, we humans do not – which is why we depend so heavily on our rules for living, rules we have to learn after birth. Compared to beagles, birds and bears, we humans are born dunces. Take birds for example. Birds are born knowing how to build their homes. No one teaches them that it's not pebbles, bones or broken glass they need to build their nests, but mud, twigs and leaves. Birds just automatically know these minor yet major details. What's more, they're born knowing how to balance nests high off the ground, to make them cup-shaped, and to build them so they don't fall apart. But we humans? We humans are born knowing zip about building our homes. We don't even leave the womb knowing how to throw up crude lean-tos to huddle under when we're in the woods and it's pouring with rain.

Like birds, bees too provide great examples of the kinds of nifty behavior patterns we poor humans aren't born with. For example, bees are born knowing not only "bee language," but also where to find their food and which "roads" to take to get to it. From birth bees understand how to locate honey-making flowers, then how to navigate back to their hives, and, once there, how to explain to their mates the exact route back to the honey flowers (they do a dance that communicates both direction and distance). In contrast, no human is born knowing language – unless we learn it from other humans, we never acquire it. Neither are we born with inner radar pointing the way to survival items – food, grocery stores, hospitals, and so forth. No, we're forced to learn from scratch everything from A to Z that we need to know to survive.

To sum up, here's what to remember about culture: It is your golden set of rules for living that are (1) learned, (2) shared, (3) coordinated, and (4) inherited from Grandma, Grandpa and all others who came before you, back to the beginning. When our species lost its instincts, it was culture that saved us. Without culture our species would fall flat on its face, would have no chance of survival whatsoever. In one sense, you could say we're all prisoners of the cultures we're born into. On the other hand, with culture every single thing any human figures out at any point in time, can be dropped into the pot holding the sum total of all human knowledge, a glorious collection of information passed on down the line, through the generations, one idea building on the last until we end with a species that can fly to the moon.

In general, cultures are slow to change. Over time, yes, both French and British cultures have changed, but French culture has done so in sync with a distinctive French formula set in motion in the distant past, and British culture has moved in sync with a distinctive British formula. To one degree or another all cultures change – but slowly, and as determined by a set of basic ideals, concepts and patterns laid down in the past.

So if cultures resist change, how did the world end up with a jellybean-bowl full of cultures, all colors of the rainbow, some as different as night from day? The answer has to do with time and geographic space. When a group of humans wanders away from its parent group, losing contact with the parent for centuries on end, this results in a new and different culture. Depending on the kinds of environmental forces it faces and the amount of time it's lost contact with its Mom or Pop culture, the offspring group will differ from Mom and Pop to a greater or lesser degree. For example, the common ancestors of Europeans and Asians parted ways hundreds of thousands of years ago, so Germans resemble the Japanese and Chinese far less than they do Italians and Poles.

In other words, cultures do change, but about as slowly as cold molasses oozing out of a frozen bottle. I believe, however, that brand-new cultures can pop up with stunning rapidity, and looking as much like their parent group as watermelons resemble green string beans. I believe it is this extremely rare kind of rapid culture change that sliced us Americans, Europeans, Chinese, Incas, and other state societies off from our healthy indigenous cousins several millennia ago. In short, our distant ancestors were infected by a strain of culture that popped up among long-starving peoples like the Ik.

Although our 4000 BCE starvation-culture ancestors resembled the Ik, unlike the Ik they were totally alone on a vast, dusty desert for generations – totally isolated, in other words, from normal healthy people. As a result, these Ik-like ancestors created a brand-new, for-the-long-haul culture, one that not only allowed violence and selfishness but actually praised and celebrated both as supreme virtues. They passed on this permanent way of life from one generation to the next, like clockwork.

In contrast, during the time they were starving, the Ik enjoyed contact with neighboring, non-starving groups. Eventually the Ik were rescued from their ugly situation, and after a few generations of good nutrition they seem to have bounced back to healthier ways. In sum, as a group, the Ik did not starve as long as our ancient 4000 BCE Mesopotamians, and Ik children seem to have eventually learned healthy ways from healthy neighboring groups.

Who were these starving ancestors? Where did they come from, what were they were like, and how exactly did they become so unforgivably ugly? In the next section we'll explore answers to all these questions.

Chapter 6

Our Ancestors Starved

> One of the most striking climate changes of the past 11,000 years caused the abrupt desertification of the Saharan and Arabia regions midway through that period. The resulting loss of the Sahara to agricultural pursuits may be an important reason that civilizations were founded along the valleys of the Nile, the Tigris, and the Euphrates. (American Geophysical Union, 1999)

Give or take a few centuries either way, around 4000 BCE a strange thing happened: for the first time in human history people chucked their relatively idyllic way of life to live packed like sardines inside the walls of the world's first cities. For most of the twentieth century these first Mesopotamian cities were hailed as the "cradle of civilization," a giant leap forward in the march of human progress. But the more we discovered about these early civilizations, the clearer the picture became. Today we know that instead of shining beacons on a hill, these early jam-packed living sites were cesspools of disease, poverty, inequality and brutality.

But archaeologists know that the inhabitants herded inside these walled-off places originally hailed from peaceful, non-violent towns where everyone was more or less equal, and where no one starved or went without. So why would people suddenly abandon Nirvana to live in squalor under the thumbs of a few violent ogres? By and large social scientists assume military conquest was involved. But many experts today insist that war didn't really exist before 4000 BCE – and certainly not wars of conquest. As we saw earlier, some indigenous people wage war to steal food, land or property from their neighbors, but never to conquer or enslave their neighbors. Only state societies slash and burn their neighbors so completely that they can totally strip away their neighbors' freedoms.

So the question remains: why would any group suddenly exchange Shangri-La for a life of crippling poverty under the thumbs of a few nasty blokes living in the lap of luxury and wealth? Although it's unlikely any group would accept such an unequal exchange willingly, it seems unlikely too that any group in 4000 BCE would have had the inclination, knowledge or tools/weapons to force others into slavery – and almost overnight.

No one has served up answers to this question that pass even the most rudimentary of smell tests. This chapter is an attempt to change that. I maintain that the answer rests on the relatively new recognition that the earth shuddered through a severe bout of climate change around 4000 BCE, one that caused a fourth of the earth's land mass to deteriorate into bone-dry desert. This caused hundreds of thousands if not millions of the world's first farmers to starve to death. A few hung on for generations, starving in extreme isolation, and eventually morphing into violent, psychotic peoples who behaved much like the long-starving Ik described in previous chapters. Their behavior solidified into a new culture, a new permanent way of life. Over the past 6000 years, these "starvation-culture" peoples increasingly dominated others, through violence and warfare, spreading their way of life around the globe.

We behave like the Ik because certain of our ancient ancestors not only starved for several successive generations, but starved while cut off from the rest of humanity – from people who could have provided healthy role models for their children. Through cultural transmission, these ancestors bequeathed their bizarre behaviors to their children, who bequeathed them to *their* children, and so on, down the line. But this kind of phenomenon is extremely rare. Throughout history, most starving groups fail to infect their children with ugly starvation behavior, simply because most starving communities live near groups that aren't starving. These healthier groups continually provide children in the starving groups with normal, healthy human behavior to copy. While Turnbull lived among the Ik, the younger women prostituted themselves with men outside Ikland (their only recourse if they wanted to remain among the living). This fact alone meant the Ik had constant input from outside, intact cultures. In other cases, non-starving neighbors adopt and retrain children from starving communities, so that the bizarre behavior of their parents fails to perpetuate.

The nineteenth-century American pioneer Donner Party is an example of a group that starved but failed to pass on their aberrant behavior to their children. In late October, 1846, the 87-member Donner wagon train found themselves trapped during a blizzard high in the Sierra Nevada Mountains of California, a storm that in some places dropped an incredible ten feet of snow. As they rolled into the mountains the Party was already low on food, and once there their hunting luck ran out. After eating their horses and cattle they chewed on boiled hides, and crunched charred horse and cow bones between their teeth.

After half the group starved to death, the living began devouring the dead. When rescuers found survivors in late February of 1847, they also found scattered around their camp human bodies, "disarticulated and butchered." And George Donner's hired hand, Jean Baptiste Trudeau, admitted to eating from the body of Donner's four-year-old nephew (Schablitsky, 2012).

But Donner-Party adults didn't pass on their starvation-induced behavior, because after being rescued their children grew up in San Jose and other California towns with normal, healthy adults to imitate and learn from. As mentioned before, unlike the Donner Party, the people responsible for our modern starvation behavior starved in isolation, and for generations in isolation. All around them, in all directions, lay mile after mile of empty, unpopulated desert land. Generations of their children had no behavior to emulate except the aberrant behavior of the psychotic adults surrounding them on all sides.

The Chemistry of Starvation

So what kinds of damage does famine dish out onto the human body and brain? Starvation crushes the body through a variety of avenues: emaciation, edema, marasmus, kwashiorkor, parasitic infestations, and infectious diseases like malaria, measles and TB. As a matter of fact, in famines people die less from starvation than from disease, which can rush like wildfire through groups not getting their daily quotas of vitamins, minerals and proteins (DeMeo, 1998: 78).

As for the psychological effects of starving, children conceived by starving mothers are twice as likely to develop schizophrenia. We know this through studies conducted in two separate countries on opposite sides of the globe: Holland and China. At the end of WWII, when Nazis hacked off their food supply, Holland suffered through "The Dutch Hunger Winter," and in the 1950s, while it was switching to communism, China too endured severe famine, with 30 million Chinese starving to death from the spring of 1959 to the end of 1961. Long-term studies in both China and Holland indicate an increased risk for famine children to suffer schizophrenia. And Dutch studies showed that adults conceived during the 1944–45 famine faced an increased risk of developing "schizophrenic spectrum personality disorders" as well as "congenital anomalies of the central nervous system" (Islam, 2016; Susser et al., 2008; Hoek et al., 1998; Harder, 2005).

Ireland too provides evidence that famine produces mental illness. In the nineteenth century the Emerald Isle was scoured by crushing poverty. If peasants were lucky, they lived in windowless one-room mud huts, often huddled together with their pigs. And this was the good news. The unemployed sheltered in poorly-drained bog holes or under roofs cobbled together over ditches. Unfortunately, most of the Irish diet at the time consisted of potatoes. I say "unfortunately," because in the 1840s a ship from North American sailed into Ireland carrying a fungus which eventually rubbed out almost the entire 1846 potato crop. After the fungus sailed in, famine lingered in Ireland for almost a decade. From 1845 to 1852 alone 2.5 million Irish souls were lost to starvation, starvation-related diseases, or emigration. As bad if not worse, a generation later the number of mentally ill in Ireland rose like a helium balloon snapped from its moorings. Before the Potato Famine hit, Irish mental institutions housed only 1600 residents total, but as famine children reached adulthood over ten times that number – 17,000 – were isolated in institutions. Another 8000 were designated "lunatics at large" (McDonagh, 2013).

Professor Oonagh Walsh, an historian at Scotland's Glasgow Caledonian University, believes future research will shine a light on a connection between Potato-Famine maternal starvation and subsequent high rates of Irish mental illness. According to Walsh the effects were epigenetic (passed on for a certain number of generations through genes, but not encoded permanently in DNA) and lasted a century and a half. If Walsh is right, and assuming 20 years per generation, this is seven and a half generations during which mental illness was passed on from Irish parent to child (McDonagh, 2013).

To refresh your memory, schizophrenia is a brain disorder causing sufferers to lose their moorings, to lose touch with reality. In short, schizophrenics see and hear things that aren't there, believe things that aren't true, and can confuse TV, movies and dreams with reality. They often foul out trying to read social cues, often isolate themselves, and are prone to strange responses – laughing during a sad movie, for example. You might see them sitting staring into space, no matter what's happening around them. While only one in five schizophrenics are aggressive or violent, those showing conduct disorder as children are twice as likely to become violent adults (NIMH, 2007).

Of course, not all cases of schizophrenia waltz out of famine epidemics. Starvation is only one source of mental illness. But among the 4000-BCE starving farmers wandering alone in the brand-new Afro-Asian desert, mental illness would be a pressing problem – if, that is, their group survived more than a generation or two. What's more, the longer a group hung on, the more likely most of its members would be crippled by mental illness. And those children who dodged mental illness – what about them? No one in groups starving for several generations would have rubbed shoulders with any humans outside their geographically-isolated group for three, four or even more generations, meaning children would grow up imitating the only behavior they knew. Psychotic behavior, in other words, soon became the norm.

A reminder: starvation culture is not only an American or European phenomenon. Through the millennia starvation culture has gobbled up much of the globe, so that to one extent or another, most people in most countries today muddle and suffer through starvation-culture ways of life. As we'll soon see, it didn't use to be this way. Evidence is good that although at one time almost everyone lived healthy lives like the Semai, Mbuti, !Kung and Inuit (Flannery and Marcus, 2012), through the millennia starvation culture gradually swamped out most of the world's healthy societies.

The 5.9 Kiloyear Event

Around 4000 BCE, give or take a few hundred years in either direction, much of the fertile green land farmed by some of the world's first farmers shriveled up into gray desert land. This was the beginning of what one researcher (DeMeo, 1998) calls "Saharasia," a gargantuan finger of desert land starting at North Africa's Atlantic coast, and sliding all the way across what is now the Sahara Desert, then Saudi Arabia, then Central Asia, and on to China. It stops just short of China's Pacific coast.

The driving force behind the birth of Saharasia was something called the 5.9 Kiloyear Event, a high-speed change in climate that was one of the most devilish aridification events in the entire 12,000-year Holocene Epoch, the modern geological period we live in today. Although the earth had plodded through other dry spells throughout the Holocene, it had always bounced back. During the 800 years following the 5.9 Kiloyear event, however, 4000–3200 BCE, a scrap of recovery occurred, but then things just got dry as a bone again.

Although no one knows what caused the 5.9 Kiloyear Event, chances are solar variation, shifts in North Atlantic Ocean currents, and changes in monsoon activity were all involved. These weakened annual rains, turning croplands into dust and desert almost overnight (Brooks, 2010: 45). But causes aren't important here. What's important are the grotesque effects that the 5.9 Kiloyear Event dropped on hundreds of thousands of ancient farmers suddenly scrambling to find food and water for their plants, animals and kinspeople. Before we travel further down this road, however, pull out a pencil and mark each of the following true or false (some you should nail instantly, since we've talked about them earlier in this book):

1. Warfare is avoidable; humans do not possess genes making war inevitable. TRUE____ FALSE____

2. War has always been with us, from the beginning of human history. TRUE____ FALSE____

3. Some human societies are peaceful and nonviolent. TRUE____ FALSE____

4. Asians are different from Europeans only because of genes

and biology. TRUE____ FALSE____

5. In most important ways, the first civilizations were colossal advances for humankind. TRUE____ FALSE____

Answers

1. True. Humans are not "born violent"; we know this because many non-violent societies all over the world live nice, quiet peaceful lives.

2. False. Before around 4000 BCE endemic warfare was unknown, and many societies even today do not do war. Institutionalized warfare – war involving standing armies, war budgets, and a warrior class, the purpose of which is the conquest of neighboring groups, including confiscation of their land, people and other resources – was unknown before circa 4000 BCE.

3. True. Many indigenous societies, including the Semai, the Mbuti, the Inuit and others, are almost totally non-violent. See peacefulsocieties.org for more.

4. False. Most of what makes any group of people different from any other is culture: learned, shared, patterned behavior transmitted from one generation to the next. Otherwise all humans are 99.9% genetically the same (Fitzgerald, 2014: 49).

5. False. We know now that the first civilizations were cesspools of human degradation: grinding poverty, slavery, disease, and endless warfare, systems locked in place to a great degree by a few thugs who used violence or the threat of it to hold onto power.

To understand the second half of this book, you must totally digest the questions and answers above. To say that humans are born violent, or that war is an inevitable human curse, is nonsense. And what makes us apples-from-oranges different from people in other places is much less about genes than about culture: the way we've learned from the adults around us how to think and behave. What's more, the first civilizations, the first cities, born first in Western Asia, then Egypt, then China, were giant leaps backwards (unless, of course, you consider grinding poverty, back-breaking slavery, festering disease and widespread warfare the picture of human progress).

Chapter 7

Before 4000 BCE, No One Was Bad

Before we tackle what happened to our early farmer ancestors hit by the horror that was the 5.9 Kiloyear Event, we need to picture who these farmers were, exactly, before their farmlands dried up into dust, stones and debris. Around 4000 BCE the major human group in Western Asia were the Ubaids. Many experts agree that before around 4000 BCE the world knew little social hierarchy, poverty, war, or human-on-human violence, and all of the above was true of the Ubaids.

In the past, anthropologists thought ancient humans were probably a lot like apes: violent, self-centered, and divided into brutish alpha males on the one hand, and females, offspring, and "weaker" males on the other. But the more evidence archaeologists uncover, the clearer it becomes that this is not so. Archaeologists find scant evidence of human inequality, poverty or violence before around 4000 BCE – and certainly none of the perpetual warfare and slavery that suddenly pop up afterwards as fast as backyard mushrooms.

But unlike the Semai and other modern peaceful peoples, most 4000-BCE agriculturalists enjoyed fertile land as far as the eye could see, with no one to drive them off it. To survive, most sane peoples left today live in hostile places too wet, cold, dry or high to grow food easily, since war-besotted starvation-culture people stole their "easy" land long ago. The Inuit live in the ice-covered Arctic tundra, the Mbuti deep in an African jungle their neighbors are too afraid to enter, the Semai inside a Southeast Asian jungle, and the !Kung in the Kalahari desert.

From around 8000 to 4000 BCE, ancient agriculturalists were fruitful and multiplied (before around 10,000 BCE farmers did not exist – we all hunted game and gathered wild berries, nuts, grasses and birds' eggs for a living). Since they lived healthy, well-fed, satisfying lives without having to worry about poverty-stricken, mentally-ill addicts breaking into their homes for drug money, or PTSD-suffering ex-soldiers blasting away at their families with semi-automatic assault weapons, I'll call these early farmers the "Smart People."

The Smart People in Mesopotamia

It was archaeologists who named the 4000-BCE Mesopotamian farmers/Smart People "Ubaidians," or "Ubaids." This name was adopted from a low mound, or "tell," where the first Ubaid remains were found. Only six feet high but as big around as 28 American football fields, Tell al-'Ubaid sits about halfway between Baghdâd and the head waters of the Persian Gulf. In the Middle East a mound is a telltale sign of an ancient city, town or community now buried under desert dust and debris. In 4000 BCE, Tell al-'Ubaid was an island rising roughly three feet above the Mesopotamian marshes, but today it sits on desert land surrounded by a barbed wire fence set onto concrete posts. Discovered in 1919 by archaeologist H. R. Hall, most of Tell al-'Ubaid was excavated three years later, by Britain's Sir Leonard Woolley.

Woolley didn't find much at Tell al-'Ubaid – it was later excavators who told us most of what we now know about the Ubaid people. He did, however, unearth a small clay statue of a woman wearing a necklace and "drapery," and part of another human figure either wearing "breeches" laced down the front, or heavily tattooed – Woolley wasn't sure which. He also found pierced earrings (nose rings?), and a clay model of a canoe-like boat with a "curled prow."

At Tell al-'Ubaid, Woolley dug up hoes, baked-clay sickles, "sledges" for thrashing grain, and mortars for grinding grain into flour, showing that the Ubaid people were some of the world's first farmers. He also unearthed thin-walled, exquisitely decorated pottery, which he trumpeted as the finest in Mesopotamia until – remarkably – the Arab conquest, some 4650 years later (Woolley, 1965: 23).

Even today, however, the Ubaids remain a mystery. Although they had the rudiments of writing, we haven't deciphered it yet, so what we know about them comes from their physical remains. Nevertheless, we do know that before they disappeared, they lived in multi-roomed brick homes with staircases, insulation, waterproofed roofs, drain pipes, central hallways, and floors made of wood, brick, or packed earth. We know they all lived in the same kinds of houses – no one had it any better than anyone else. Their architecture was so sophisticated that they almost certainly used advanced math to build it, including the Pythagorean Theorem (Charvat, 2002). "[W]e now know how 'Ubaid architects worked in the era before blueprints: they built a scale model one-tenth the size of the final building, giving their bricklayers a template to follow" (Flannery and Marcus, 2012: 278).

Ubaid people were family-oriented. Children were found buried with jewelry, tiny ceramic cups and jars, and food to eat on the journey to the afterlife (children's graves held small animals while adults were entombed with whole joints of meat). As each family member died, the family grave was reopened to accept the newly deceased. This grave might have been opened first for Dad, then Mom or a child who died young. Sometimes graves were opened for family pets. In one Ubaid grave a fifteen-year-old boy was buried with his dog, bone in mouth, and stretched across the boy's lap (Leick, 2001: 12). Ubaids kept salukis, greyhound-like canines with long ears and silky coats, a dog the ancient Egyptians called the "royal dog of Egypt" (Egyptians used salukis to hunt gazelles).

Among Ubaid remains archaeologists have found bone whistles, and "a suspected mouthpiece of some blown instrument" (Charvat, 2002: 59). What other musical instruments did these Smart People play? Since most were probably made of wood, skin, and other perishables, Ubaids could have entertained each other with entire orchestras filled with drums and cymbals, wind instruments like the flute, and stringed instruments like the harp (with strings of hair, plant fiber or animal gut).

Above all, the Ubaid people were smart. Ubaids invented much of the technology that in the past has been credited to their starvation-culture conquerors, the Urukians, originators of the world's first "civilization." Take writing, for example. Ubaids "must... have seen the birth of at least the graphic versions of some of the signs of earliest Uruk culture writing systems" (Charvat, 2002: 111). In other words, starvation peoples only improved upon the basic, world-shaking concept of freezing sound-language onto clay tablets or prepared animal skins.

Ubaids were also probably first to invent metallurgy and to make bronze; "...arsenic bronze of copper, which was to dominate Mesopotamian metallurgy for at least a millennium to come, first appeared in the upper Euphrates area in the Ubaid period" (Charvat, 2002: 81). Although archaeologists haven't dug up much metal at Ubaid sites, what they do find to be common as pebbles on a beach are whetstones: the tools that shape metal into other tools, art, jewelry, and more.

We now know that the Ubaid people were also experts at weaving and cloth production, and that they probably invented the weaving loom long before the first cities and "civilizations" stood up on their hairy hind legs: "If the excavators of Tell Awayli [an old home of the Ubaids] identify the loom weights from their site correctly, this is the first moment in history when the weaving loom, representing a fairly sophisticated machine, appears on the archaeological horizon" (Charvat, 2002: 82).

Ubaids were also some of the first on the planet to ride around in animal-powered wheeled vehicles, and they did so long before starvation-culture bullies created the first cities at Mesopotamian cities like Ur, Uruk, Eridu and Susa. Judging from the explosion of cow bones found in late Ubaid sites, the Ubaid people might have ridden cowback, too, in addition to harnessing cows up to wagons and sledges. And sea-going vessels? Probably; a clay model of a ship was uncovered in a Late-Ubaid cemetery at the ancient Mesopotamian town of Eridu on the Euphrates River near the waters of the Persian Gulf (Charvat, 2002: 87).

Of Ubaid beliefs we know painfully little. Clues to their religion, however, lie in their clay female figurines, Barbie-doll thin, with women's bodies, reptilian heads, and tall, cone-shaped hats, crowns or hairdos. When archaeologists dig up half-human, half-animal figurines like these, they all agree they've uncovered deities. With impossibly wide shoulders and improbably narrow hips, these figurines are often trimmed out with dots, lines and chevrons – clothing decoration, tattoos, or reptile markings? We don't know. Sometimes these figurines carry babies, suggesting they are Mother Goddesses. The babies feature the same slanted, flat, slit-eyed faces of their mothers.

Another clue to Ubaid religion: Ubaids buried their dead in bottomless brick boxes or in pits dug directly into the ground. This at least was how all 193 of the bodies excavated from the Ubaid cemetery at Eridu were buried (Leick, 2001: 12). In other words they were "laid to rest" in direct contact with Mother Earth, who apparently, in their minds, posed no threat to them, and was possibly central to their belief system.

Most amazing of all, Ubaids shouldered none of the ugly baggage carried by their conquerors: poverty, snobbery, slavery, hunger, yada, yada, yada (Frangipane, 2007; Descartes, 2018). "No archaeological evidence has been found [at Ubaid sites] attesting to great differences in political power, wealth, or prestige" (Descartes, 2018). Archaeologists have failed to find evidence of these ills among the Ubaids, until their end times, when they were being infiltrated and overcome by starvation-culture bullies, and when their way of life was beginning to blend in with the sick starvation-culture way of life. Before then, the

Ubaid people lived in a kind of Garden of Eden. Unfortunately, they were about to get kicked out of the Garden – not by Jehovah or Yahweh, but by cold-blooded swamp creatures modern archaeologists call Urukians.

The 5.9 Kiloyear Hit Fast and Wide

> The evolution of the earliest complex state-level societies and cities from small sedentary communities took place in southern Mesopotamia between 8000 and 5000 cal yrs BP during the "Ubaid and Uruk" periods. *Attempts to explain this transition often discount the role of environmental change...* (Kennet et al., 2006).

Around 4000 BCE – roll the disaster music, please – the 5.9 Kiloyear Event skewered the world, including the Ubaidian Garden of Eden. The result? A huge hunk of the earth's land mass quickly turned from fertile green fields into bone-dry wastelands of sand, dust, and rock. This wasn't small-potatoes change, but a "major reorganization" of the world's climate – the last major change, in fact, before today's. "[I]t appears that the 6th millennium BP represents a key transitional period during which the global climate underwent a major reorganization... this was a widespread and systematic reorganization of the world's climate" (Brooks, 2010: 51, 44). Ironically, even though it coincided with a major U-turn in human history – the birth of cities, civilization and the state – the 5.9 Kiloyear Event hasn't been studied as well as the climate shifts that struck before and after, i.e., around 6200 and 2200 BCE.

The 5.9 Kiloyear Event probably came on like gangbusters. Many believe it was an example of "Rapid Climate Change," or RCC, a shift in climate so fast and furious that it drastically disrupts both humans and the environment, and is noticeable "over timescales on the order of a human lifetime" (Brooks,

2010: 43). And it hit not only Africa and Asia, but the entire globe. Researchers have recorded evidence of the 5.9 Kiloyear Event from Tanzania, Venezuela, the US, Peru, Germany, the Himalayas, New Zealand, the Andes, and Ireland (Brooks, 2010: 49).

You should keep two key facts in mind, here. How quickly the 5.9 Kiloyear hit, and how large an area it sliced and diced. This climate revolution dried out enough land so fast that tens of thousands of human beings suddenly found their homelands too shriveled up to keep them alive. Human communities were zapped in one of four ways:

One: some died out in short order.

Two: some were close enough to large rivers and other bodies of water to relocate.

Three: others spent generations wandering around wastelands, isolated, starving, barely alive, sometimes finding oases that lasted a few years before drying up. Unless they eventually stumbled upon a large body of water, most of these died out too.

Four: after starving for generations, one or two of the groups in "three" above stumbled upon an oasis with a permanent food supply. But by this time the group had morphed into a society like the Ik's, with people arranged in hierarchies based on age or physical strength, hierarchies kept in place through violence.

More about these four different groups – and especially the last – is coming up in the next chapter.

Chapter 8

The Birth of Starvation Culture

Where It Happened

If you could blot out Iran, the Middle East would look like a simple oblong box of sand, walled off from the world by mountain chains and sea walls. Turkey's mountains form the northern wall of the sandbox, and Iran's mountains and the Persian Gulf the east wall. The Arabian Sea is the southern wall, and the west wall is formed by the connection of the Red and Mediterranean Seas. And the area inside the box? It's mostly dry-as-a-bone desert land, consisting of the Al Khatim Desert near Abu Dhabi, the Al-Dahna in Saudi Arabia, the Nefud in the north of the Arabian Peninsula, the Ramlet al-Sab'atayn in Yemen, the Wahiba Sands in Israel, and the Judaean Desert covering both Israel and the West Bank. The Rub' al Khali or "Empty Quarter," is the largest sand desert in the world. It blankets a goodly portion of Saudi Arabia as well as parts of Oman, Yemen and the UAE.

When it comes to drinking water, the Arabian Peninsula today is a stingy old miser. Nearly empty of lakes and rivers, its main sources of drinking water are its ancient aquifers, some of which have burst forth to the surface to create oases, and its "wadis," stream beds carrying water – but only in the rainy season. To find non-toxic drinking water and fertile soil on this Peninsula, your best bet is in getting to Mesopotamia, the "Land Between Two Rivers" (Tigris and Euphrates) or to one of the few oases blooming in the desertland.

But before around 4000 BCE and the 5.9 Kiloyear disaster, the Arabian Peninsula was wet and productive, with people living even in its interior. "Significant populations" of farmers kept goats and sheep, fished, periodically raised cereal crops, and lived along the Persian Gulf and also in the interior of the

Peninsula, along lakes, springs, creeks and rivers that have since disappeared (Kennett, 2006).

Although archaeologists are beginning to realize how important the Arabian Peninsula is to our understanding of human population movement and its connection to the environment, so far the digging they've done there is miniscule. So we don't know a great deal about 4000 BCE on the Arabian Peninsula (which belongs mostly to the giant country of Saudi Arabia, but also to Yemen, Oman, Qatar, Bahrain, Kuwait, the United Arab Emirates, and parts of Jordan and Iraq). However, archaeological sites explored in the UAE and Oman show that desertification began blistering those areas around 4000 BCE, and that most settlements went belly-up at the same time. The 1000 years that followed are called the Arabian "dark millennium" – because humans seemingly abandoned the Peninsula. It wasn't until around 3000 BCE that they returned to the interior of Saudi Arabia (Max Planck Institute, ND).

As mentioned in the previous chapter, most of the 4000-BCE sandbox communities probably starved to death in short order, before even one generation could raise offspring and create the next generation. Imagine you're living in the middle of the fertile Arabian Peninsula around 4000 BCE. This place where you live is the size of the continental American West: 1,200,000 square miles. And then imagine that suddenly, several summers in a row, the rains completely abandon you. The lake your community lives on totally disappears, and the nearby rivers and streams do too. Everyone's goats and sheep die, their grain shrivels up and blows away, and dead fish blanket river and lake beds of dried mud as hard as nails and riddled with crazed crack lines. You can't even hunt wild game or gather wild plants like your ancestors did, because those animals and plants too need water to survive.

What will you do? Yes, water surrounds you on three sides: to your west lies the Red Sea, east the Persian Gulf, south the

Arabian Sea. All great for salt-water fishing. But try drinking salt water next time you're at the shore – I guarantee it will not quench your thirst. Drink enough of it, as a matter of fact, and in no time flat you'll be dead from dehydration.

Even if you know where the nearest drinkable water is (and you don't), the most your group can travel is 10–20 miles a day. So salvation is weeks or even months away, over and across deadly spans of waterless desert. And even if you had a bonanza of food and water stockpiled to carry with you on your journey (you don't), you'd survive only a few weeks on the road before running out. In the best of situations humans can survive three days without water, at most a week, but yours is not the best situation – you're walking all day long, over land so hot you could fry eggs on the rocks you pass (if you had eggs, which you don't). Not to mention the fact that you were thirsty and dehydrated even before the journey began.

Some rivers, of course, were large enough to survive the 5.9 Kiloyear's brutal pummeling. The Tigris and Euphrates were probably the only two large enough to fit into this category. The Ubaid Smart People already living on these two rivers survived, as did Ubaid groups near enough to them to reach one before their group went belly-up. And so, the banks of the extremely large rivers, like the Tigris and Euphrates in Mesopotamia, and the Nile in Egypt, were soon flooded with refugees running from the fast-expanding wasteland forever creeping up behind them like the Devil with gaping jaws. These are still the same people they've always been, however, peaceful, egalitarian sharers – as mentioned earlier, I like to call them "the Smart People."

Starvation Culture as an Embryo

The third group of Smart People fleeing the devastation all around them were the least fortunate. Instead of reaching fertile, well-watered land, or even dying off quickly (which would have been a relative blessing), this third group wandered for years in wastelands barely fertile enough to feed rats and cockroaches, let alone humans. Never quite dying out altogether, they eventually morphed into people resembling the Ik. Beating off others any way he could, the strongest man gorged on any and all food the group found. After gorging, he might toss a few scraps to those who kissed his feet. This kind of magnanimity happened rarely, but it was worth "kissing up" for the occasional bits that would end up in your belly versus someone else's.

These groups suffered not only from the existential effects of never having a secure food source, but also from the biological and psychological effects of bad nutrition. Such communities would be full as ticks with problem behavior – people tone deaf to the needs of others, unpredictably violent, hearing voices, seeing ghosts, believing nonsense, and so forth. It would be like living in the psych ward of a major metropolitan hospital – with no sane person hovering around anywhere enforcing rules or limits.

After a few generations no one alive in these groups would remember anything but psych-ward behavior, nothing but people behaving more like rabid animals than human beings. Animals, however, protect their young, but these starving humans didn't have enough mental or physical health to do the same. As with the Ik, anything weaker than you – even your own children – was seen as a liability, a threat. Prolonged or repeated famine has the effect of allowing emergency behavior, patterns essential to survival in the midst of a crisis, to become normalized. This apparently occurs because younger members of society grow up knowing no alternatives. Colin Turnbull felt he witnessed a pivotal moment among the Ik of Uganda when memories of food sharing died with the last members of the society who could recall what life was like in the absence of famine (Dirks, 1994).

So after a few generations, children born into what I'll now call embryonic starvation culture had to wrestle with psychotic adults. On top of that, many of these kids were born with their own mental problems. Remember: we now know children conceived by starving mothers are twice as likely as others to develop mental illnesses such as schizophrenia. As with the twentieth-century Ik, the core motivation for these ancient psychotic adults was food – nabbed by any means necessary: stealing, subterfuge, lies, even murder – didn't matter, as long as you ate.

Such groups would probably have begun to use hunting weapons to maim or kill other humans. For this group, gone are the days when people shared food equally with their neighbors. As with the Ik, in starvation culture the person everyone wants to be is the cunning con man, the one who can murder while feeling nothing, the trickster who can lie, cheat and steal with a clean conscience – and without getting caught. As Colin Turnbull discovered when he lived with them, the Ik ridiculed their "friends" for trusting "friends," and respected only those who hurt others, only thieves and con artists (Turnbull, 1972: 245, 248, 249).

The Permanent Oasis

I believe even most incipient starvation-culture groups eventually went belly-up. Groups in which parents murder their own children to avoid sharing food with them suffer comparatively low survival rates. However, I think a few of these incipient groups eventually stumbled upon oases large enough to sustain them for the long haul, with an abundance of sparkling clean water, figs, dates, wild meat, and other edibles. Even today several oases still pepper the Arabian Peninsula. On the Persian Gulf side, the Qatif and Al Hasa oases lie in northern Saudi Arabia, and Liwa is located in the United Arab Emirates. On the Red Sea side of the Peninsula are Qurayyah and Tayma; east of the Mediterranean Sea in the Levant, are Azraq and Ein Gedi.

At the oasis, the incipient starvation-culture group is now

food-rich, and can feed itself twice over. But will it return to its old Smart-People ways? No. No one now alive remembers the old ways, or believes the stories told by their now-dead grandparents. Like the Ik, even when good times bounce back, sick behavior reigns supreme. Turnbull said that even after they began to eat well the Ik still maintained their damaged behavior (Turnbull, 1972: 270, 280ff). Today the Ik, along with certain other observers, say they no longer exhibit the repulsive characteristics Turnbull observed when he lived with them. If this is true, the difference that allowed the Ik to recover while the incipient starvation-culture groups did not, lies in the fact the Ik live close to other, healthy communities while the starvation-culture groups in 4000 BCE were totally isolated. In other words, Ik children eventually had healthy behavior to learn from, emulate and imitate whereas starvation-culture children did not.

Although there's now enough food for everyone, to the starvation-culture person it never *feels* like enough. What's more, the starvation-culture person has learned an entirely new set of cultural behaviors, most erupting out of the heart-numbing fear of never having enough: lying, cheating, stealing and violence as high goods; social stratification as something handed down from the gods, with the most cunning and successful takers on top, the weak at the bottom (the sick, the old, slaves, women, children, the crippled, the maimed), and everyone else perched on various intermediate rungs of the ladder.

So even though the group is physically healthy now, it still behaves as it did when it was stark-raving mad from hunger. Anthropologist Robert Dirks notes that "Hunger and famine often condition profound transformations in culture (i.e., changes in food habits, forms of government, and magical and religious practices)" (Dirks, 1994). One of the first things group members probably did with their new-found leisure time was manufacture hunting weapons for killing the wild animals that flocked to the oasis for the same reason they themselves did:

the oasis is gushing with food and water. From there, it's only a hop, skip and a jump to the idea of turning those weapons on each other.

After all, it's thieves and the most cunning thieves who are most admired by these people. And what better way to steal than by using a hunting spear to threaten a woman weighed down by a back full of ripe figs and prickly pears just picked from the trees on the far side of the oasis, if she fails to surrender her fruit? Killing others for food certainly wasn't frowned upon during the desert-wandering days of extreme starvation – and it isn't now, either.

It's important to remember that four to five generations earlier, these ugly individuals more or less resembled the gentle Smart People introduced earlier in a previous chapter. Back then they would have felt guilt at the idea of stealing from another human, let alone killing one. The notion of killing another human being – especially just to get food you didn't need – would have been anathema. As it is today among the Semai of southeast Asia, chances are that even the notion of hitting another person was unthinkable to the great, great grandparents of these incipient starvation-culture adults. But the old culture that harbored Semai-like values was lost now, replaced by one that substituted psychotic morays, ideals and behavior for the morays, ideals and behavior of the idyllic ancestral past.

The idea of using hunting weapons to maim or kill fellow humans was probably first hit upon by one lone individual – the way the concept of the wheel probably occurred first to one lone individual skilled at thinking outside the box. The idea of killing other people might even have begun with "games" in which humans hunted each other for sport, or competed with each other the way ancient Roman gladiators competed. The Ik, remember, found pleasure in only two activities: eating, and watching others suffer.

Now that our incipient starvation-culture group has stumbled upon the Oasis, they feel no overwhelming physical urge to eat (although the psychological need is still strong), but interest in entertainment circling around human suffering will still be as strong as ever. And with a sudden bonanza of spare time on their hands after reaching the Oasis, our group could quickly become antsy and bored without some form of entertainment. What's more, their new culture dictates that the only satisfying form of entertainment involves watching others get hurt. As noted in a previous chapter, this urge to ogle suffering is still with us today, and is satisfied by sports like football, wrestling, boxing, hockey and dog fighting, and by violent films, TV shows, internet porn, snuff films, etc.

So one way our Oasis group used their new-found leisure time could very well have been by inventing new kinds of hunting weapons, crafting hunting weapons, practicing with these weapons, using the weapons to hunt animals that came to the oasis to eat and drink, and inventing games in which their only form of entertainment – watching others endure pain and suffering – could be satisfied.

But our budding starvation-culture group probably used their leisure time in other ways too, like exploring the lands around them, wandering further and further away from the oasis, curious to see what lay beyond the horizon. Also, even though the head honcho still considers eating and watching others suffer his main pleasures (a la the Ik), he's now physically healthy and finds he doesn't mind sexuality nearly as much as his starving grandfathers did. So the oasis population mushrooms. Although the head honcho still hoards food and women, like Atum of the Ik he worries about the day when someone wilier than he is will make mincemeat out of him.

Birth of Starvation Culture

So at last we're looking at the birth of pure starvation culture, born when the random, psychotic, time-bound behavior of starving people has been shaped into a permanent set of interlocking behavioral patterns exhibited by essentially non-psychotic individuals. The force that keeps starvation culture alive – potentially ad infinitum – is culture: learned, shared, and patterned behavior passed from one generation to the next, on and on and on through time. Most of us never question our own cultures. It never crosses our minds to do anything our culture hasn't taught us, and even if it did, public opinion keeps us from straying very far at all from our particular cultural norms.

The core motivational belief scissoring through starvation culture is a subconscious, fear-based belief that enough is never enough. Not enough food, not enough money, not enough stocks and bonds, not enough gold squirreled away in the attic. Don't throw away those old penny loafers! The bottom might fall out of things next year, and you'll need those old shoes! No matter how much you possess, you're somehow nervous about the probability of coming up short.

I believe this core belief was handed down through countless generations to us today, and that it explains much about ourselves that has heretofore remained unexplained. It explains, for example, why billionaires move heaven and earth to find a way to slurp up yet another billion. Doesn't matter how many billions they're already sitting on, or that they'd be unable to spend even half their wealth if they lived another 200 years, they are certain they're not safe until they mop up another X number of billions (if nuclear war or climate change ravages the Earth, who'll be on the short list to move to those new artificial environments we plant on the moon? I don't have nearly enough billions to make it onto that list! I need more, more, and more, because who knows how many I'll need when the time comes!).

Erase It and Replace It

What happened in the Middle East 6000 years ago wasn't a matter of one culture simply morphing into another. It wasn't like the French becoming British in a few generations, or the Chinese suddenly turning into the Zulu of South Africa. Because, of course, that could never happen. Not today, anyway; the world is too interconnected. No, there was an in-between step, an "erase-and-replace" process that allowed one kind of culture to suddenly morph into another totally different culture, as different, in fact, as night is from day.

This erase-and-replace action begins with a culture being wiped out – erased in other words. And by "wiped out" I don't mean the people themselves, but their rules for living. When an ancient Saharasian group starved for so many generations that it had begun to look like the sickest wing of a major metropolitan psych ward, that's when we're looking at a culture-less group. Even at a permanent oasis, such people remained culture-less things at first, akin to rabid animals, with individuals walking around the oasis dazed, grabbing food from others and gobbling it ASAP, snapping and snarling at each other.

Picture the Ik on steroids.

But at a healthy oasis, the children in such groups could pig out on an abundance of healthy food. And so, from this bedlam, the group's now physically healthy children, over the next few generations, eventually organized the psychotic behavior of their parents into a brand-new patterned culture. The only problem was, these new rules for living were what one might find among the Ik, or in a hospital for the criminally insane.

This new way of life was passed down through the generations like buckets of water handed from person to person in a fire brigade. Oasis people were not allowed to behave idiosyncratically or randomly, but were expected to "obey" the group's new norms the way people in every culture must do (if you don't, you're poked fun of, shunned, locked up, driven away or executed, depending on the severity of your transgressions). For example, western culture demands that western men willingly serve in the military during times of war, and if they don't they risk being scorned – or worse. Likewise, in our newly formed 4000-BCE desert oasis culture, those who suggested that stealing might be wrong? They too would have been scorned – or worse.

To sum up, in some 4000-BCE groups caught in the violent climate change swept in by the 5.9 Kiloyear Event, the old Smart-People way of life was wiped away to nothing. And this vacuum opened up the way for a brand-new, upside-down culture to waltz in and take over. Bizarre and extremely harsh, yes – but learned, shared, and patterned so as to allow humans to survive together in groups without killing each other each and every day of the year.

In the next chapter we'll look at exactly how a 4000-BCE lala-land, starving group might have reacted as they stumbled upon a permanent oasis after starving for generations on the Saharasian desert. For now, however, it's important to understand that this erase-and-replace process is critical to understanding how such a crazy, shoot-yourself-in-the-foot system like starvation culture could have gained a toehold in the first place, and how such a destructive way of life could have replaced the relatively idyllic Smart-People way of life almost overnight.

Chapter 9

Starvation Culture Grows Up

> [D]espite being the most far-reaching political development in human history, the origins of the state and what determines the age of statehood are still not very well understood. (Ang, 2015)

In the last chapter we witnessed the birth of starvation culture, a grotesque new way of life formed around 4000 BCE when humans were caught like rats in a trap in a gigantic, rapidly expanding desert. Although most groups caught in the ballooning desert died out, a few spent several generations in isolation, starving and barely clinging to life. After finding their way to permanent oases, others were driven away by those who'd beaten them to the punch, gotten to the oases first. A handful of groups, however, stumbled onto unoccupied oases and survived there permanently. Although the chaotic, random behavior of a bedlam group would continue, succeeding generations would be well nourished from that point on.

A group sicker than the Ik suddenly let loose on a permanent oasis buried under tons of luscious food and clean, clear drinking water – think Garden of Eden – might have looked something like the following description, which is based not on archaeological evidence – we have no such evidence for the Arabian desertlands from this time period – but on my own best guessing based on what is known about starving people.

At the center of everything would stand the group's strongest male. We'll call him Alpha. Alpha might be as thin as a pencil, totally dehydrated and covered in lice, scabies and fleas, but everyone – men, women, young people, children – were careful to avoid him like leprosy. Everyone had seen Alpha rip his obsidian knife out of his belt and slice men almost in two with it – often for no reason anyone could see. What's more, the very last thing anyone did was look at Alpha while he ate.

Alpha gorges until passing out, and falls into a murderous rage when he sees others eating. However, since food is as free as air now, others do eat – but in secret, and after Alpha's fallen unconscious. After all, they've spent their lives eating alone, in secret, to keep others from snatching the food out of their mouths, so this is just the same old, same old. (Among the twentieth-century Ik, children pried open elderly mouths, removed the food, and popped it into their own little mouths, and the elderly were too weak from starvation to do anything about it.)

If food was left over after Alpha gorged and fell to the ground in a stupor, it went to the woman Alpha favored at the moment, and everyone knew not to bother Mrs. Alpha either, while she ate. Alpha tolerated a few adult males – those he could count on to pick, gather and kill food and bring it back to him untouched. In some part of her feeble, psychotic brain, each woman in the group longed for the day when Alpha would elevate her to the top of his "my favorites" list. The women in Alpha's group, all of whom were sickly upon first arriving at the oasis, sometimes bore live children, a few of which actually survived. Some women would nurse a new baby and even carry it for a few years in a sling over her back. But as with the Ik, once babies reached a non-cuddly stage mothers chased them away.

Alpha Whips Up a Private Food Storehouse

Eventually, however, when crazy Alpha discovers others eating "his" food, he throws up a sticks-and-stones structure to cram with stored food, all the while snarling and raging at others for eating. For his entire life Alpha has been tortured by fear that food will run out, and at any moment he will starve to death. Even a permanent food supply fails to clear that fear from his fevered brain.

But how to protect his food cache? When Alpha leaves to snare a rabbit for lunch, someone might very well smash into his storehouse. For a while Alpha's brain works overtime, and finally he comes up with a plan: he needs an ally to guard his food, a chump who will guard the food but not eat it, someone wily as a desert fox, yet still fearful of him, Alpha. So he strikes a bargain with the second-strongest man in camp: "Help me keep it safe and I'll share my food with you." As we'll see later, sharing a bit with an elite few is key to the survival of the state. Without such largesse, the state would wither away. Today, for example, while starving the vast majority of his people, Kim Jong Un is very careful to keep a small elite well fed, smiling, and smothered in international luxury goods.

Like the Ik, Alpha's people find pleasure in almost nothing but eating and watching others suffer. This too fails to change just because they reach a permanent home. The strongest regularly beat up the weakest – just for the fun of it. The "good person" is the one best at lying, cheating and stealing – and getting away with it. Blood sports become the rage. Human-on-human weapons are invented.

The Birth of Social Inequality

Once they reach the safety of the oasis, Alpha Male and his new buddy-guards terrorize others into snagging food for them. This isn't much of a change either from how things transpired on the desert. Back when the group was wandering aimlessly, then too Alpha held everyone tightly under his thumb. And here's where we see the birth of social hierarchy, of snobbery, of groups divided into the worthy versus the worthless, con men vs the duped, rich vs poor, strong vs weak, young vs old, male vs female, jock vs non-jock, and so on.

Over the next few generations Alpha's group exploded in size. The nutritious food made everyone feel sexy again, and women gave birth constantly. In the old days, Smart-Culture women spaced their births four or five years apart, but in Alpha's group women had no say in anything. In fact, women were downright despised – by men, children, other women, and even themselves. After all, women were physically weaker than men. Worse, Smart-Culture women were identified with Mother Earth, and in the eyes of Alpha's group, Mother Earth had abandoned them all, Her children. The Mother-Earth Goddess (curse Her name) had dried up into a wizened old hag.

Not only that, everyone in Alpha's group was born of mothers who kicked them to the curb at age three or so. Mothers who snapped and snarled if children came within ten feet of her food. Mothers who snatched food out of their tiny hands, stuffed it into their own mouths – right in front of them, and with a nasty grin on her face as she munched and enjoyed the sight of their tiny sad faces and the sound of their stomachs growling. So no one had much use for starvation-culture women – not even the women themselves.

Since men cracked on women for sex constantly, whether women wanted it or not, women were constantly pregnant. And because the oasis bristled with all kinds of nutritious food, food women could pick and catch on their own and sneak into bushes to eat, their babies grew up physically healthy. Girls began bearing babies as soon as they were physically able (and served as sex slaves before that). In other words, this grimy group grew and grew.

As time went by, Alpha took on a few more buddy-guards, and although they didn't get a giant's share of Alpha's tools, weapons, gizmos and women, they did get more than others got. Alpha's buddy-guard system, however, turned out to have one large drawback for Alpha: when he was a few years shy of forty, his strongest buddy-guard murdered him in his sleep, becoming Alpha2, the new man serving to strike terror into the hearts of the group. And a few years later Alpha3 managed to slice and dice Alpha2. Meanwhile new buddy-guards had to be scouted out to guard Alpha3's storehouses, so bloody axe battles were held, with winners scoring buddy-guard status. Well, the long and short of it was, a few elites soon ran the show, and everyone else served as stepped-upon slaves, or beasts of burden – scrappy with each other, but never with their "betters."

After a number of generations at the oasis, something huge happened to Alpha's group. It didn't seem so at the time, but this event would end up changing the history of the world.

Starvation Culture Travels

Eventually something happened at Alpha's oasis that would change everything from then on into the far distant future. It was this: Alpha's group stumbled upon the peaceful Smart People, or Ubaids, living the good life at the Tigris and Euphrates rivers. Maybe Alpha teenagers took to roaming the desert for adventure, or to burn off excess energy, or just for something to do. As time went by, they would venture further and further afield, and it was inevitable that at some point they would run into the beautiful people at the Rivers.

Or maybe it was the other way around. Maybe Ubaid travelers stumbled upon the oasis, and spun marvelous tales to Alpha's people about the glamorous big-river cities. After all, as we learned in an earlier chapter, Ubaids stood worlds ahead of Alpha's people. Since Ubaids had learned to irrigate the land around the Fertile Crescent, they dined regularly on an amazing array of cultivated vegetables, grains and fruits. Over time they had trained magnificently talented chefs and created a variety of cooking arts and mouth-watering cuisines. From their domesticated herds they feasted on a number of milk products and tender cuts of meat. On top of all that, they boasted a wealth of beautiful art, architecture, clothing, jewelry, furniture, musical instruments, and other artifacts that would take Alpha people's breath away – literally stun their senses.

Starvation Culture Strikes It Rich

If you're thinking that Alpha's starvation-culture people, when they discovered the riches at the Tigris and Euphrates Rivers, asked nicely to share some of the culinary delights, the fabulous clothing, the sparkling copper jewelry, or the fine art lavishly spread inside Ubaid homes and civic buildings, think again. Remember: to Alpha's people the "good" man is the one strong enough to take whatever from whomever, whenever, wherever and however he can.

Ubaids at the Tigris-Euphrates River communities didn't stand a chance. Since they had no need for human-on-human weapons, they owned none. Neither did they know how to make, use, or succeed with this new kind of "tool." In contrast, Alpha's people had been inventing, producing, perfecting and practicing with human-on-human weapons for quite some time. What's more, Alpha's people had no qualms about using such tools to maim and kill their fellow humans. In fact, they were like the Ik in enjoying watching humans suffer, so asking nicely for things would have spoiled their fun. Much more exciting to rip the goods straight out of the hands of the peaceful Ubaids – and knock a few heads together if and when any protested.

You might think the Smart People could have fought the starvation-culture people with their farming, butchering and hunting implements, but like the present-day Semai, their hearts, minds and souls were probably as fit for killing human beings as modern Westerners are for killing their pet cats and dogs. They had no mindset for it, no psychological preparation, no physical or mental training for it. They had no practice working together in armed and coordinated human units for the specific purpose of killing other humans. They had no skill in the art of killing others while avoiding being killed by those they would be trying to kill.

For those of us living in starvation-culture countries, it's difficult to imagine people who've never engaged in human-on-human violence, using guns, knives, tanks, landmines, missiles, and other weapons designed specifically for that purpose. Even harder to imagine: people who wouldn't know how to use such weapons even if they were placed directly in their hands. Yet this is true of the Semai today, and before about 4000 BCE it was probably true of, not all, but almost all human groups on the planet.

By the way – this 4000-BCE clash between the crude and violent Alpha culture and the gentle-yet-sophisticated Smart People could never happen today, since over the past 6000 years the violent cultures have wiped out all the gentle sophisticated ones. Today most peoples tend to be either gentle and unsophisticated (I give you the Semai, Mbuti, Inuit and others), or sophisticated and violent (I give you the developed nations). A third combination, violent and unsophisticated all wrapped up in the same smelly package, is rare these days – I give you the Mongol "hordes" and the Huns of historical fame.

Alpha People Pay a Visit to Their Smart-People Neighbors

When starvation-culture people first visited the wealthy, mentally healthy groups at the Tigris and Euphrates River delta, my guess is they had a field day gobbling away at the amazing food, trying on the gorgeous tunics and mind-blowing jewelry, banging away with sticky fingers on the percussion instruments, and blowing away with sticky lips on the wind instruments. Anyone who got in their way would probably have been summarily shoved to the ground. And at the thought of returning to their oasis and spinning tales about the fantasy land they'd discovered, they of course loaded up on every marvelous item they could carry, in preparation for a show-and-tell session back home. They might even have loaded up on several Ubaid humans, as beasts of burden if nothing else.

This first "neighborly" visit between Urukian Alphas and

Ubaid Smart People opened up the floodgates. Over the next few years increasingly large excursions left the oasis for the River delta, to binge on, and plunder the riches there. It was only a matter of time before starvation-culture people realized they didn't have to return to the oases, they could just move into and take over whichever River-delta building they fancied, forcing the owners to act either as henchmen, or slaves. As this new trend evolved, the oasis was eventually abandoned, and starvation-culture people increasingly controlled the larger, fancier homes and buildings in Ubaid Smart-People communities.

The starvation people of course brought their way of life with them into the non-violent Mesopotamian communities, in all its ugly glory: their great joy at watching others suffer; their deep and overwhelming need to hoard everything in sight, not only food but all the physical objects they could lay their hands on – whether they belonged to them or not; their division of the human group into a few elite males at "the top," with everyone else dumped into slave status at the bottom; and last but not least their eagerness to earn the praise of their fellows, which could be achieved only by being the best lying, cheating con artist in the neighborhood who could also steal more things than anyone else and get away with it scot free. Remember the Ik of Uganda.

With this 4000-BCE merger of the violent Urukians and the peaceful Ubaids we come to what has been hailed as the marvelous "birth of civilization" in the "cradle of civilization," the birth of the state in the Tigris and Euphrates River valley. Actually, as we'll see in the next chapter, this merger was, for the most part, rot and horror galore.

Chapter 10

Crazy Town: The First "Civilizations"

And so it was that the first "civilization" was born in Mesopotamia, "the land between the rivers," the great Tigris and Euphrates. First, the alpha male left the oasis to move into the richest Smart-People settlement in Mesopotamia. Second, he took over the largest building as his living quarters, and moved his buddy-guards into nearby homes already occupied by Ubaid home owners. Third, after conning, manipulating and terrifying enough Ubaid people into becoming his "guards," Alpha commanded sufficient armed warriors to turn the city's Ubaid citizens into abject slaves who produced clothing, tools, weapons, jewelry and other goods and services inside the city. Alpha let other Ubaids live outside the city to till the fields and raise the sheep, cows and goats. Everyone though, field tillers and city slaves alike, gave all they produced to Alpha, who hoarded it, doling out just enough to keep people able to keep on keeping on.

Contrary to popular opinion, the first civilizations were anything but bright and shiny Gardens of Eden. For starters, citizens were packed like sardines in a can inside city walls, most dirty, hungry, poor and sick. William A. Haviland, Professor Emeritus at the University of Vermont: "[E]arly cities were disease-ridden places with relatively high death rates… Dense population, class systems, and a strong centralized government created internal stress… Warfare was common; cities were fortified…" (Haviland et al., 2013: 270, 273). Perhaps even more appalling, at the ancient Mesopotamian city of Ur, Sir Leonard Woolley uncovered "death pits" with up to 75 individuals buried in the same underground chamber as one alpha male or female (at this point in time – 2600–2450 BCE – both sexes apparently could become alpha bullies, and thus attach a multitude of others with them as they journeyed into the afterlife).

For the first time in history thousands were packed inside walls alongside human and animal excrement, leading to unhappy results: TB, bubonic plague, typhoid fever and cholera. Sunlight and fresh air kill tuberculosis germs, so when TB-infected country people coughed, air and sunlight burned away any TB microbes hanging around to do damage. But in the early cities TB bacteria grew like corn in Kansas, hopping rapidly from one warm body to the next through the dark, dirty spaces inside urban walls.

For the first time too, institutionalized social classes reared their ugly heads. No longer was one person as good as anyone else. Instead, people were now sifted into social piles, with one pile as golden as the gods, and others full of losers no better than the refuse dumped over the cities' walls. In short, this was a sudden, gigantic leap backwards, from healthy human groups into societies filled with both physical and societal sickness. The eminent political scientist and anthropologist James C. Scott goes so far as to say that it was good when the early Mesopotamian and other city states collapsed – which they often did – because for most of their inhabitants these cities were nothing but dangerous, depressing and oppressive places. Scott suggests that people everywhere are better off after their state societies break up into smaller constituent communities (Scott, 2017: 208 ff).

Sir Leonard Woolley, the British archaeologist who excavated the Mesopotamian city of Ur, gave me my first taste of one of the world's earliest cities. Woolley's excavations at Ur rank "as one of the most important archaeological finds of all time," right up there with Howard Carter's 1922 discovery in Egypt of King Tutankhamun's tomb (Baadsgaard et al., 2011: 28). Actually Tell al-Muqayyar (mound of pitch), Ur is situated in modern Iraq about halfway between Baghdad and the Persian Gulf. Today the remains of the city lie about ten miles west of the Euphrates River, but in its heyday, Ur was a bustling harbor city perched on the banks of the River (which over the millennia has changed course).

For twelve winters between 1922 and1934 Woolley dug around in the Mound of Pitch, but even after these twelve seasons he and his team of hundreds of Arab workers examined "only a minute fraction of the city's area." Nevertheless, they uncovered Ur's temple quarter, parts of its residential and commercial centers, and its tombs – both royal and "common."

It was Woolley's description of Ur's Royal Tombs that has stuck with me through the years. Dating from Ur's First Dynasty, the Royal Tombs were crammed with items made of, or smothered with, gold, silver and precious stones, especially carnelian and lapis lazuli. Ur's elites buried themselves in these tombs with gold helmets, gold wigs, gold hats, gold oxen reins, gold statues, gold-encrusted harps, with silver hair ribbons, pins and makeup kits, daggers with solid gold blades and jewel-bedecked handles, jewel-studded clothing, and much, much more.

Of all the items Woolley dug out of the royal tombs at Ur two of the most famous and remarkable Woolley called "rams in a thicket." These are a set of lifelike goats sculpted out of gold and lapis lazuli (an indigo-blue gemstone) that served as matching end tables for Ur's upper crust. The goats are standing completely upright, on hind hooves, with their front legs entwined in a golden tree or flowering bush. The goats are stunning, with eyes, horns and beards of polished lapis lazuli, and other body parts sculpted out of limestone, gold and silver. Until Wooley's excavations at Ur, the world had assumed (judging from later Babylonian and Sumerian remains) that early Mesopotamians were a crude lot, with little style or sophistication. The refinement and wealth Woolley uncovered in Ur's Royal Tombs, however, put that notion to rest for good (Sayce, 1930: 276).

The Royal Cemetery of Ur

But what intrigued me most about Ur's Royal graves were not their glamorous, exotic grave goods, but the extra human bodies discovered in them – bodies that should not have been there. In "the Great Death Pit," for example, over 70 dead bodies, in "the King's Tomb" 63 extra bodies, and in Royal tomb 1050, 40 unaccounted-for complete sets of human skeletal remains. And to make things even more mysterious, no one knows exactly who these individuals might have been before their bodies ended up in someone else's grave.

Woolley stumbled upon the Royal Cemetery immediately outside Ur's city wall, in – of all places – the city's rubbish heap. In Ur it was common practice for citizens to lug their trash to the top of the city's eight-foot-tall wall and pitch their refuse over and out of sight. Eventually, quite a pile of cured garbage rose up outside and attaching itself to the wall, and after several generations, Ur's dump had grown into a mound of inert earth many feet high. By the time the first Royal tomb was dug, around 2600 BCE, this mound provided more than enough room for burial pits. (When Leonard Woolley measured the basal width of Ur's wall, it measured at its narrowest 82 feet – the length of an American high-school basketball court – and in some places it was a whopping 30 feet wider.)

Not all of the graves in Ur's wall-side cemetery were royal. Of the 1850 tombs excavated by Woolley and his team, the vast majority were small, simple ones containing solitary individuals and a scattering of their worldly belongings. But 16 graves were sumptuously elaborate and filled not only with the deceased individual and his/her stupendous riches, but also with the extra dead people, all of whom died simultaneously with the individual to whom the grave belonged.

Boasting the most extra dead people was Royal Tomb 1237, "the Great Death Pit." Roughly the size of a small twenty-first-century American movie theater (24′ by 27′), the Great Death Pit was built with mud-plastered walls hung with reed mats over the plaster. Lining the wall immediately inside the door of the Great Death Pit were six soldiers with weapons (knives or axes), and in front of the soldiers stood a large copper pot ringed with the bodies of four women harpists, "one with her hands still on the strings of her instrument" (Moorey, 1982: 76). The body of the big cheese to whom this burial pit belonged had disappeared – probably stolen or destroyed by tomb robbers.

In addition to its guardian soldiers and harpists, the Great Death Pit also held the bodies of 64 women stretched out in neat rows and dressed in short-sleeved scarlet jackets with lapis lazuli, gold, and carnelian beadwork sewn onto the cuffs. Woolley suspects the red jackets were held closed by silver or copper stick pins. On their heads the women wore hats resembling upside-down bowls as big around as lampshades and smothered with stemmed flowers, tree leaves, and rings made of gold, silver and shell. Gold beech-leaf pendants dangled from each hat. The 64 female bodies were also bedecked with crescent-shaped gold or silver earrings the size of doughnuts. Some women also wore belts made of rings carved out of shell, and all wore beads around their necks, ribbons wrapped several times around their hair, and what Woolley called "dog collars," made of gold and lapis lazuli.

Rivaling the Great Death Pit for its number of dead bodies, tomb 789, "the king's tomb," contained 63 human skeletons, including six helmeted soldiers with spears, three drivers of two ox-drawn chariots, and 54 other men and women. Royal tomb 1050 contained 40 bodies, and tomb 800, "Queen Puabi's tomb," contained three bodies inside the Queen's chamber (a separate room inside the burial pit), five men guarding the ramp dropping down into the pit, and 10 women playing musical instruments (Wesler, 2012: 91).

Because Ur's death pits were carved out of the earth before narrative writing was invented, we have no texts explaining why they were chock full of human bodies. Who were the people buried with Ur's elites? Did they consider themselves fortunate – or residents of the bottom of Luck's barrel? We know some were chariot drivers, soldiers, guards, harpists and lyre players, probably the best musicians, military men and drivers the Big People knew. But who were the others? Personal servants – valets, chamber maids, slave overseers, accountants, butlers and the like? Were some the friends of the elites, or trusted storehouse managers? The most talented graphic artists in the realm? Were some concubines?

And when did these sacrificial humans breathe their last? Evidence suggests it was after the deceased elites were laid in each tomb and surrounded by their regalia. At that point the doomed musicians, soldiers and others would trot down a ramp into the pit and find their pre-ordained places to stand or sit. Someone must have orchestrated everything, making certain everyone was in their proper places.

But did the sacrificed die willingly, or go out kicking and screaming? Were they murdered, or did they die peacefully and voluntarily? One clue: next to each body in the Great Death Pit Woolley found cups, making him think the deceased were poisoned. But did they drink at the point of a dagger – or cheerfully? Although the bodies are laid out in neat rows with no sign of struggle, the grand orchestrator of the show might have dropped down into the pit after the poison had worked its magic, to tidy things up. On the other hand, another chilling possibility is that the retinue did not suspect they would be buried in someone else's grave, but were told they would enter the pit only to give the deceased a ceremonial send-off to the afterlife. Maybe they assumed the poison they drank was merely an innocent glass of fermented barley brew.

In 2011 University of Pennsylvania researchers uncovered new evidence that throws Woolley's death-by-poison hypothesis into question. Upon examining a male and female body buried in two different royal graves at Ur, the researchers found a remarkably neat, round hole 30 mm in diameter punched into the woman's skull. In the man's head were two similar holes. For those of you bad at measurements, these are holes as big around as a US half-dollar.

This data, of course, suggests that both individuals died from blunt force trauma to the head, which in turn suggests that Ur's death-pit retainers might have died not from poisoning, but from head wounds made by a peculiar weapon light enough not to crush the human skull, but heavy enough to knock a tidy, round hole in it. What kind of weapon would that be? Right away we can eliminate spears, daggers, swords and lances from the running. Also out: axe heads and stone mace heads, which instead of piercing a skull would crush it. The answer might lie in a singular weapon Woolley unearthed in one of the royal graves: a copper battle axe roughly eight inches long and spiked on one end (Baadsgaard et al., 2011: 36).

Still, Woolley found cups next to the extra royal-grave corpses – perfect for holding poisoned liquids or sedatives. Was everyone sedated and stretched out on the pit's floor before receiving blows to the head? This method would be much easier than having dozens watch others die one by one, knowing their turn was coming – no muss, no fuss, less blood to clean up afterwards, fewer cups and other paraphernalia broken in the panic that almost certainly would have ensued if a courtier lost his nerve and spread terror like an electric current through the group. On the other hand, Ur's Big Cheeses at this time were starvation-culture bullies, and for them human suffering was prime-time entertainment.

At no other time in Mesopotamian history do we find such bizarre mass burials as we do in Ur's Royal Cemetery. We do find other cases of human sacrifice in early Mesopotamia. In two 3000-BCE graves at Basur Hoyuk and Arslantepe in southeastern Turkey, a few teenagers were thrown in alongside high-status individuals, in apparent cases of ritual sacrifice (Jarus, 2018; "Arslantepe", 2015). But here again, writing hadn't been invented yet, so there's no one to explain to us what was going on here. Was it "Where I'm going, I'll need servants," or "They're mine, no one else can have them"? Or perhaps, as suggested above, it was simply the psychotic "need" to salivate at the thought of human suffering – of family and friends of the murdered, in addition to that of the victims themselves.

Although the above is astonishing, it's not surprising. In Ur's 16 royal graves are two extremes – artistic magnificence on the one hand, and human cruelty on the other. But this is just what one might expect at the initial intermingling of what was possibly the world's first psychopathic culture with the healthy one that had reigned supreme up to approximately 4000 BCE. "[S]uch collective burials are unknown anywhere else in Mesopotamia (excepting a possible reference in a text from Lagash) either before or after. Much about them remains puzzling" (Horne, ND). But perhaps not puzzling? While Smart People knew how to whip together fine food, fine dining, fine art, and fine everything else, the starvation-culture bullies who enslaved them knew how to turn people into domesticated cattle. If these two vastly different peoples were combined into one group, we might well expect the kind of monstrosity uncovered in Ur's otherwise sophisticated royal tombs.

The Temple Cloth Weavers

But it wasn't just human sacrifice that seared itself into my memory banks as I read Woolley's *Excavations at Ur*. One other thing still haunts me: Ur's Third-Dynasty temple "workers." I put "workers" in quotes because Woolley makes them sound more like animals than women. By the Third Dynasty, scribes recorded not only everything that flowed in and out of Ur, but also where it came from, so we know that in one building in Ur's "Temple Quarter," 165 women and girls sat slaving away making cloth. Some picked dirt and straw out of wool sheared from the backs of sheep outside the city wall, others spun the wool into yarn, and a third group wove it into cloth. All 165 women were paid with a daily food allotment, and apparently nothing else.

The grotesque part of this was the amount of food each woman received, which depended on three things: how much wool, yarn or cloth she produced, the quality of her work, and her age. The more and finer her product, the more she was given to eat. But her daily ration also depended on her age, so that if an adult got four pints of oil a day, say, her child got three, two or one, depending on its age. And elderly women? Like the youngest child of all, old women got only a pint of oil a day.

We treat dogs better today. Woolley calls the temple-women arrangement "cold-bloodedly businesslike" but I call it starvation culture. Although Woolley doesn't say, my guess is, along with food the temple workers might have been doled out some of the clothing they made. If so, it was no doubt woven from the scratchiest, least expensive wool Ur's sheep had to offer. Apart from the above few facts and conjectures, we know little about Ur's temple women. Did they sleep where they worked? Were they free to come and go? Or were they, like harem women, locked 24/7 inside their temple work rooms?

By 3000 BCE, the city of Uruk, situated northwest of Ur by about 65 kilometers, had 40,000–45,000 inhabitants. Of those, 9000 were temple-cloth women, definitely slaves (Scott, 2017: 158). Mesopotamia had lots of great soil for growing food, but was dirt-poor in metals, minerals, and other raw resources, so it had to trade for these. And the major thing they traded for these resources? Cloth. The textiles made by the temple-cloth women and girls. Where did these women come from? Most were apparently captured in war, but others were probably widows, the wives and children of debtors, the indigent, orphans, and abandoned children.

The New Slave Machine

When humans harness brand-new, previously untapped energy sources, big social changes lurk not far behind. Around 10,000 BCE the birth of plant and animal domestication led to humans settling down for the first time in history, in permanent settlements, with permanent homes, fields and buildings. It also led to a population explosion. In the nineteenth and twentieth centuries CE the harnessing of electricity and the internal combustion engine led to monumental changes in the way we travel, communicate, learn, play and work. (It also boosted the West's standard of living, and wrecked the earth's climate.)

Around 4000 BCE the first human slave machine was invented, and this amazing new energy source too led to monumental social change. Slave "banks" altered the way people worked, played and related to one another. Suddenly a top few wallowed in glittering luxury: magnificent palaces, clothing smothered in silver, gold, and gemstones, awesome entertainment, the finest food prepped by the best chefs – you name it, they had it.

At the same time, however, everyone else lived lives of unimaginable misery: laboring with scant food in their bellies until they died of exhaustion or disease, and owning almost nothing. This was the essence of the first state societies, the main tool of the starvation-culture alphas: a mass of thousands of humans roped together and forced to work as one, giant, unified machine. The sole purpose of this new energy source was to produce a surplus of everything for the power elite. And you'd better believe the power elite guarded their new machine with red-eyed jealously – it was the magic charm staving off their starvation-culture fear of never having enough.

Early Mesopotamia "was, in a very profound sense, a world without free men" (Scott, 2017: 156). From around 3000–2500 BCE Babylonian slaves belonged to temples or rulers, and lived in crude barracks in labor camps. At that time those in the temples were the unluckiest slaves of all, since unlike household slaves, they could not be bought or sold. Nor could they buy their own freedom.

Babylonian slaves left their barracks each morning in gangs for labor-intensive work under overseers' watchful eyes, and were quickly punished for even small infractions. In the city of Uruk, scribes used the same age and sex categories for slaves as they used for animals. One might presume, therefore, that in the eyes of the Uruk elites, slaves were "domesticated" humans, "wholly equivalent to domestic animals in status" (Scott, 2017: 159).

But we're getting ahead of ourselves. Let's return to the fourth millennium BCE, when starvation-culture Urukians have just begun creaming the Smart-People Ubaids. We know little about these final Smart People because as the conquered, they morphed into the lower classes, and archaeologists tend to focus on ruling-class winners versus lower-class "losers." A few scholars, however, are beginning to complain about the lack of attention given to the ordinary people of the fourth millennium BCE, and are working to remedy the situation.

One such scholar is Reinhard Bernbeck, of the Department of Anthropology, Binghamton University, New York. Bernbeck believes Urukian-Era "subalterns" (low-status persons; subjugated Ubaids) endured hideously miserable lives. Workers, he says, were "victims" who suffered. As people acquainted with human freedom and equality – they'd heard old stories passed down from ancestors – subalterns had to be tortured into surrendering their freedoms. According to Bernbeck, labeling the switch from Ubaid to Urukian the "birth of civilization" is a monstrous misnomer; more accurately it was "the genealogy of enslavement and alienation," and "the advent of public repression" (Bernbeck, 2009: 57).

Remember: because the Ubaid-to-Urukian switch happened before true writing was invented (the Ubaids were just beginning to invent it at this point in time), our information about the switch springs from art and other objects (buildings, statues, walls, tables, chairs, spears, helmets, dishes, jewelry, etc.) left by those who suffered through this agonizing period. Fortunately, thanks to little items called "cylinder seals" we have loads of art from the time. Cylinder seals were ancient locking devices and picture IDs. Small ones were about the size of your thumb, while the largest measured up to four inches. These little devices were made of metal or stone, and were bored through lengthwise so they could be looped with a leather thong and worn around your neck or wrist, for ease of use.

Here's how cylinder seals were used as ID and locking devices. First, seal carvers carved unique pictures belonging to you and you alone into your cylinder seal. Second, by rolling your sealstone over wet clay, you sliced your "signature" into that clay. Third, you then slapped the wet clay onto your bottle of wine, chest of gold, bushel of barley, or whatever. The clay was positioned so that after it dried no one could open your bottle, chest or bushel without breaking the clay.

On your cylinder seal you could carve anything from goats, boats or flowers, to temples, people or thunder gods. Although Ubaids used seals for quite some time before Urukians latched onto them, the latter ushered in their own special brand of seal images, such as people in "unequal relation" to one another. Another Urukian artistic innovation: pictures of "violent class conflict" etched into their sealstones. According to Mr. Bernbeck, Urukians were probably first anywhere to toss such conflict into their art (Bernbeck, 2009: 46, 57).

The First Pictures of Human Inequality in History

On one Urukian cylinder seal two naked men are torturing four others. "Torture" is Bernbeck's word, not mine (Bernbeck, 2009: 51, 52). The torturees, also naked, seem tied in knots: bound hand and foot, arms tied tightly behind their backs, their thighs are pressed flat against their chests, calves pressed smack against thighs. At the right end of the squat picture frame, another naked man kowtows to a giant in a calf-length tunic.

Brandishing a sharp-tipped spear as tall as he is, the giant quietly watches the action, the paddle-shaped lobes of his hat dangling several inches below his chin (or the hat could be hair, it's hard to tell). The torturers hold stick-like instruments over the bound men, ready to let their cudgels drop. On the ground two men sit with their arms yanked back, shoulder blades stretched impossibly close together. A third man leans on the fronts of his knees, calves, and feet, with his knees drawn to his chest and his head lowered to the ground. A fourth appears to be suspended by his hands from something that isn't shown – maybe a horizontal bar or a tree limb.

According to Bernbeck, although this and similar images are usually labeled "war scene," they are not war scenes at all, but portrayals of "the repressive forces of an emerging state against its own population." The damning evidence: if the armed men were warriors, why show them naked (Bernbeck, 2009: 51)? Bernbeck says these are the first representations of human inequality in history, and that they indicate dramatic social change during the switch from Ubaid to Urukian times. In other words, this is raw, unadulterated starvation culture cloning and spreading itself like butter over hot toast. It is starvation-culture monsters transforming Smart People into domesticated animals. Since Smart People were unacquainted with the concept of humans being domesticated like dogs, cats, goats or sheep, they had to be taught it. And those disinclined to learn? They had it violently forced down their throats.

Warty Food Bowls

Another item radiating clues about Smart People suffering through the Ubaid-to-Urukian switch, is the ugly but ubiquitous "beveled-rim bowl," that pops up in droves at archaeological sites dating to switch times. Archaeologists have, at a single site, lifted tens of thousands of the wretched things out of the dirt. One archaeologist found them lined up on the ground in neat rows as if waiting to be filled with something. General thinking is these were bowls for feeding workers and slave gangs laboring in fields or de-sludging the canals that branched out from the Euphrates River all over Urukiana, both inside and outside its city walls.

BR bowls were the warty toads of Urukian dinner ware. Misshapen, clumsily built out of the coarsest of clays, and with thick, lumpy walls, they resembled short, squat bells turned upside down. Because no one cared if these bowls were pretty or not, they could be made in a flash. Urukians knew the simple potter's wheel, but it was reserved for fashioning pottery for the "finer" folk only. In contrast, BR bowls were built by hand: after dropping a lump of clay into a hole in the ground, the potter pressed it out to the walls of the hole, and because no one wasted time trying to smooth them away, you can still see the potters' finger prints inside the bowls.

Probably pumped out on worksites by the slaves who ate from them, BR bowls seem to have been trashed after a single use. Otherwise how to explain the tens of thousands littering every Urukian site unearthed in Mesopotamia? After lunch at the worksite, diners apparently abandoned their bowls – more efficient than lugging them back to the barracks and then to a different work site the next morning (after all, workers had tools and other paraphernalia to lug to and from work sites).

In one ancient picture a human head is shown with a BR bowl pressed to its lips, making researchers think the contents of the bowls was partly or wholly liquid. Texts suggest it was a barley brew – a sort of barley beer perhaps. Reinhard Bernbeck calls it a "sticky alcoholic pulp."

As mentioned earlier, one archaeologist found BR bowls arranged on the ground in neat rows. Why? One explanation might be this: workers were not trusted to line up for food – they might sneak back in line for seconds or thirds. Instead, bowls were first set out on the ground and then filled with food, and only after that were workers allowed to trot over, sit before a bowl, and eat… one helping and one only. Our starvation-culture ancestors were as cold as vultures circling the dead.

Why Did People Chuck Their Freedom?

Some archaeologists wonder why the first Mesopotamian city-dwellers chose to live under the thumbs of a handful of backward bullies. For example, Mihriban Ozbasaran: "The pertinent question is… what induced people to give up a life of relative autonomy in favor of a way of life in which only a few people would… join the elite class…?" (Ozbasaran, 2012). Ozbasaran tries to answer his own question: "One possible mechanism... is that everybody benefited from the process in that the standard of life was raised even for commoners."

But as we've seen, the switch from Ubaid to Urukian culture did not "raise the standard of life" for commoners, whose largely idyllic lives had been turned upside down into nightmares of intense overcrowding, disease, slavery and brutality. So no, Ubaids almost certainly did not relinquish their freedoms with a shrug of their shoulders, but on the contrary must have been beaten into it. Starvation-culture Urukians had perfected the use of weapons against humans, but Ubaids had not. Second, Urukians considered violent taking-behavior admirable while the nonviolent, share-and-share-alike Ubaids did not. The rest is pure logic: enslaving Ubaids was as easy as frying eggs in a red-hot skillet.

Today a look-alike for this first starvation-culture/Urukian "civilization" might be North Korea. Under Kim Jong Un many North Koreans are starving (Martin, 2017; Silva, 2017). For them, in addition to food, healthcare, clean water and sanitation are also in short supply. For a small elite, however, who kowtow to Kim, life couldn't be sweeter. Food, medical care and clean water are abundant for these fortunate few, who can also shop for a wide variety of luxury goods – paid for in part by commoners laboring outside Korea in near-slave like conditions. Indonesian lawyer Markuzi Darusman said that 50,000 North Korean laborers are currently stationed in countries across Asia, the Middle East, Europe and Africa – with a high percentage in Russia and China – where they will sometimes work 20-hour days while provided with inadequate food, minimal time off and a monthly paycheck of only $120 to $150. They work primarily in the mining, construction and logging industries, assigned to the more dangerous tasks (Jenkins, 2015).

According to Anthony Ruggiero, formerly with the US Treasury and State Departments, "...the North Korean government only allows profits to go to one of three purposes – the weapons program, the military, or *luxury goods for the elite*" (Whoriskey, 2017) [italics my own]. Just like early starvation-culture bully leaders, Kim Jong Un knows his survival depends on both terrifying and coddling a small group of "buddy guards" who will slice and dice the masses whenever necessary.

During their early days with the starvation culture Urukians, Smart-People Ubaids remembered their old life, and no doubt longed for it with every fiber of their being. But after three or four generations they forgot the old ways and began to consider bowing and scraping to alpha Elites "normal" behavior. Social stratification was now fully stirred into this new blended culture, having become an unquestioned part of the learned, shared, patterned behavior passed on from one generation to the next, down through the ages.

Chapter 11

The First Institutionalized Warfare

Back in the old days, in the fourth millennium BCE, more than one Smart-People Ubaid community perched on the banks of the Tigris and Euphrates rivers. Naturally, some of Alpha's smarter henchmen abandoned Alpha to bully one or more of these other towns into submission. After all, these henchmen wanted and needed a few lowerlings of their own to bully and boss around. What's more, they certainly didn't like the idea of being bossed by Alpha for the rest of their lives if they could help it. And with these other marvelously wealthy towns nearby for the taking, they could.

Soon there was a multiplicity of Alphas, each bossing his own private Ubaid community somewhere along the Tigris and Euphrates in what is now Iraq, but back then wasn't. You can see where this is going: with an Ik-like fear of never having enough, all these Alphas were driven by an overpowering urge to take all the stuff in the community next door to them, and then the stuff in the community beyond that, and the next, and so on. Soon all Mesopotamian cities were packed inside big, thick defense walls.

Another thing that led to large-scale, institutionalized warfare was the need for warm bodies to keep everything humming along. To keep their monumental storage buildings full to brimming, starvation-culture overlords needed an astronomical number of slaves – to grow food, to process it, to raise sheep, to weave cloth to trade for precious metals and other items Mesopotamia lacked, and so forth. Women couldn't grow babies fast enough to meet the mammoth demand for slaves. "With few exceptions, the epidemiological conditions in cities until very recently were so devastating that they could grow only by adding new populations... They did this in two ways. They took captives in wars... And they bought slaves..." (Scott, 2013). Hence the necessity to sally forth, raid other groups, and drive their citizens home to add to your already existing, home-grown slave bank.

Urukians were the first Mesopotamians to wage large-scale, organized warfare, and chances are good they were first to do it ever, anywhere. Evidence of this lies among the catastrophic remains of a mysterious battle that took place around 3500 BCE at an ancient site called Hamoukar, today only a 50-foot mound shooting up from the plains of northeastern Syria. Although experts were skeptical at first, all of them now agree that what happened at Hamoukar was not an earthquake, a tornado, or a natural fire, but the "earliest evidence for large-scale organized warfare in the Mesopotamian world" (Jarus, 2010).

Why are the experts so sure it was a battle that devastated Hamoukar? For one thing, over 1200 clay bullets were excavated at the site, and at the time clay bullets were the killing tool of choice, delivered with a slingshot – the weapon David used to topple the biblical behemoth Goliath. Don't sniff at the idea of baked clay as a killer. In order to get a feel for what these weapons could do, the Hamoukar archaeologists made their own slingshots, and one excavator accidentally hit Clemens Reichel, the lead archaeologist, in the head with a clay bullet. "'The impact is quite remarkable,' said Reichel... 'He wasn't very good at that point, but by god I felt it... Once he got really good, the speed, the velocity, that those guys get is amazing... I'm virtually certain it can be fatal'" (Jarus, 2010).

What made Hamoukar a battle target? In 3500 BCE it was a large, famous tool-manufacturing site. Although it had just begun to use a brand-new tool medium called copper, it mostly made things out of a coal-black substance imported from Turkey: obsidian. When polished, obsidian is as shiny, sharp and deadly as broken glass. For years before the battle, Hamoukar had turned out obsidian tools and weapons; archaeologists found obsidian cores and chips spread over an area the size of a modern golf course.

The battle destroying Hamoukar took place 5500 years ago. From the city of Uruk, 700 kilometers north of Hamoukar, an invading army of a few hundred bombarded the walled settlement with hundreds of oval-shaped clay bullets. Some of these clay missiles were flattened on one side, suggesting that the invaders ran out of ammunition and had to manufacture bullets while the battle raged, in a clay pit outside the city walls. Apparently, the invaders were so desperate for ammunition that they shot bullets that were still wet.

At one point, Urukians broke through Hamoukar's ten-foot-thick wall and set fire to the town. They burned down its administrative buildings, bakeries and homes, reducing them to rubble. Inside one of the burnt-out buildings archaeologists discovered clay bullets lined up at the edge of what had been a basin of wet clay for making clay sealings. The roof of the building, however, ravaged by fire, had fallen in before the bullets could be used.

In the battle debris Reichel's team found skeletal remains – probably Hamoukarians killed in battle. Also buried in the rubble were hundreds of clay sealings, used to lock the Hamourkarians' doors, jars and other containers. But the most interesting thing found was a small colony of a few hundred Urukians living outside Hamoukar's walls. Reichel thinks they might have moved to Hamoukar to strike it rich. In 3500 BCE Hamoukar was not only a giant tools-and-weapons manufacturing site, it was also a manufacturing site situated on an impressive trade route stretching from Turkey all the way to Uruk City. In other words, in that day and age, it was probably one of the easier places to become rich and famous.

What has Reichel scratching his head is this: the army that marched 700 kilometers to conquer Hamoukar. It also sliced and diced its own Urukian "brothers" living outside Hamoukar's wall. When this was announced, in 2010, the headline of one article flamed brightly with the word "fratricide" (Jarus, 2010). Why would brothers kill brothers? One theory: it was an error; the invaders failed to recognize the colony as one of their own. Another theory: the invaders considered the colonists traitors. A third: since they had a good thing going and didn't want the invaders to horn in, the Urukian colonists sided with the Hamoukarians against their invading "brothers."

At any rate, a haunting mystery associated with Hamoukar is, why would men kill their own brothers? But is it a mystery? Like the Ik, Urukians seemed to have no brothers – or sisters, or parents, or blood relatives, period – none they recognized anyway as any different, or more special, than anyone else they knew. And if it meant gaining goods or power, they'd turn on their best buddies in a minute flat. In other words, viewed through the lens of starvation culture, the fratricide at Hamoukar is no mystery at all. It's simply a matter of starvation culture doing its thing: stealing what belongs to others, even from one's family – out of a fear of never having enough.

So, a few generations after the 5.9 Kiloyear Event carved a gigantic finger of desert land from West Africa to the Pacific Ocean, the world's first cities sprang up. And increasingly we're suspicious that it was the abrupt change in climate that produced these cities. In elementary school my teachers assured me that the first cities were God's shining temples on a hill, the "birth of civilization," the beginning of all things good and holy.

But we now know the truth. Early cities were cesspools of poverty, slavery, violence and disease. Slaves were doled out small allotments of daily food, and strict records were kept to regulate each allotment. When starvation-culture Alphas died in the city of Ur around 2600 BCE their things were buried with them – not only their inanimate belongings, furniture and chariots (with the oxen that pulled them), but also dozens of other living, breathing human beings who were cursed with some kind of unknown, unfortunate relationship to the Alphas.

Chapter 12

Starvation Culture Travels the Globe

Why do some societies consider "blood soup" and charcoaled grasshoppers delicacies of the highest sort, whereas others turn chalky white even at the thought of eating such rarified cuisine? Why do some societies think keeping 10 wives is just fine and dandy while others consider it the height of stupidity, immorality, or both? Why do some consider wearing feathers in one's hair the height of beauty and sophistication, while others consider feathers in the hair a laughing matter? Chalk it all up to this thing anthropologists call "culture": learned, shared and patterned behavior passed on from one generation to the next, on through to infinity (or to whenever that particular cultural group of people goes belly-up).

Cultures change, but slowly, and any new trait has to show it can "play nicely" with other traits before being allowed to join the club. Take gunpowder, for instance. After the world's first explosive was stumbled upon by the Chinese in the ninth century CE, it eventually spread all over Europe and Asia – but to certain societies only. Groups like the Semai didn't adopt it, because gunpowder didn't mesh with other parts of Semai culture. For example, since the Semai don't do war they wouldn't need gunpowder as a firearms propellant. And since they don't quarry rocks or minerals, or build roads, they wouldn't need it as an explosive. Besides that, the Semai are a gentle people, and gunpowder is about as gentle as a starving mountain lion devouring its prey.

So gunpowder had little chance of being adopted by groups like the Semai. But state societies? When gunpowder came knocking at the door of the state, it was welcomed with open arms. Starvation-culture/state societies all keep armies, all need war weapons, and all need roads for those armies to march on in order to beat the other side to the next battle site.

Human inventions come in two different flavors: on the one hand, those that were invented once and once only and were then passed around from one place to another, and on the other hand those that were invented "independently" in two or more places around the globe. Gunpowder was invented in one place and one only: China. We used to think that plant domestication and agriculture were invented in western Eurasia in two different places: Europe and the Middle East. Now, however, we know better. According to recent genetic evidence, farming popped into western Eurasian people's heads in one place only – the Middle East. Europe got farming only by stealing the idea from early Middle Eastern agriculturalists (*ScienceDaily*, 2014). Dogs, on the other hand, are the opposite: we used to think only one culture domesticated the dog, but now we think the "invention" of the dog happened twice, once in Europe, and once in East Asia (*ScienceDaily*, 2016).

The Mother of All States

I believe the state (starvation culture) was invented in one place, and one only – the Tigris-Euphrates river valley in what is now Iraq, soon after 4000 BCE. Before then, state societies existed nowhere on the planet. After its birth in Mesopotamia, the state – like gunpowder – then marched to other parts of the world by spreading from its original cradle. About 1000 years after its first incarnation on the Tigris and Euphrates Rivers, the state gallivanted south to Egypt, arriving there by around 3100 BCE. Once there it pummeled the peaceful Smart People crowded along the banks of the Nile River. After Egypt, the state dragged itself west to the Yellow River in China (Hsia Dynasty), which it reached by around 2000 BCE (Otterbein, 2004: 160). Finally, some 2000 years after it hit China, it sailed across the Pacific, and down the west coast of the Americas, where it crushed the

Zapotec people around 200 CE, in what is now southern Mexico (Otterbein, 2004: 124).

Each time one of these four new states was born, it was the same old story: peaceful Smart People with no cancerous social divisions, no poverty, and no institutionalized warfare, morphed into the opposite: ugly people constantly at war, shackled with poverty and violence, and broken into social classes with slaves at the bottom; elite rulers, priests and warriors at the top; and a few other stragglers squeezed in between. What's more, each new state ushered in a deep need to keep vast quantities of food and other goods "in the bank."

Reasons They're Wrong and I'm Right

I should mention here that not everyone agrees with me on this point. Most theorists believe that the first four early states – the Mesopotamian, Nile-River, Yellow-River, and Zapotec – each arose all by itself, without knowing anything about the existence of any of the others, and with no help from any of the others in getting started. Carneiro, for example, believes that "We can… reject the belief that the state… arose through a 'historical accident.' Such notions make the state appear to be something metaphysical or adventitious, and thus place it beyond scientific understanding… It was not the… result of chance, but the outcome of a regular and determinate cultural process… Not a unique event but a recurring phenomenon..." (Carneiro, 1970: 733).

I don't believe it. It's more likely that this elaborate complex of cultural traits arose in one place and one only, and was then foisted on various more or less peaceful egalitarian societies as time progressed. As noted above, many culture traits were invented once only, in one place, and then spread ("diffused") to other parts of the world. The wheel and wheeled vehicles seem to have been invented once and once only, in the Middle East, and from there spread across the world. As we saw earlier, gunpowder was invented in China and China alone, and then carried to the rest of the world. Complex behavioral patterns too have arisen once and once only. For example, religions such as Islam and Christianity arose in one place and one only, and were then dispersed to other parts of the world.

Time and Space Sequencing

The temporal and spatial sequencing of the four early states also support the theory that the latter three arose from the first in Mesopotamia. These four states follow each other in time like baby ducklings following their mother: the Mesopotamian erupted around 4000 BCE, the Nile-River around 3000 BCE, the Yellow-River around 2000 BCE, and the Mexican around 200 CE. After the first in Mesopotamia, the second state popped up in Egypt about 1000 years later (Fagan, 2016: 44), with Egypt being only a hop, skip and a jump southwest of Mesopotamia. The third rose up 1000 years after the one in Egypt – in China. And finally, the fourth shot up due east of China, by 200 BCE, along the west coast of the Americas, and although most social scientists don't favor the idea, the recipe for setting up this first state in the Americas could very well have floated over to the American continent on a slow boat from coastal West Asia (Fagan, 2016: 44; l). In short, this geographical and time sequence is exactly what one might expect if the idea of starvation culture/ the state were carried – on foot, later on horseback, and still later by boat – from the first Mesopotamian state to the other three pristine states.

Geographical Sequence

What's more, this time frame fits like a glove with the geographical distances between these first four state societies. From the Tigris to the Nile is roughly 1700 km as the crow flies, and considering the undeveloped nature of transportation between 4000 and 3000 BCE, it is conceivable that it would have taken about

1000 years for the brutal state system to walk itself from the Tigris to the Nile. To get from the Tigris to the Yellow River in China, the proverbial crow would need to fly roughly 6000 km, about three times as far it did to get to Egypt. So one might expect it to take about three times as long for the idea to reach China as Egypt. But it took only twice as long. Why? Because transportation had speeded up, was considerably more sophisticated between 3000 and 2000 BCE than it had been between 4000 and 3000 BCE.

Finally, to waltz the state from China to the Americas, my guess is that starvation-culture bullies carried the idea in boats via the North-Pacific and California Ocean Currents, from Japan to British Columbia – roughly 7500 km. At British Columbia the North-Pacific Current veers south and becomes the California Current, which follows the coast of California down to Baja California. Then, from the tip of Baja, it's only about 1300 km, as the crow flies (still hugging the coast), to Oaxaca, Mexico, home of the Zapotec. It makes sense that it might have taken 2200 years for seafaring technology to get good enough to execute this trans-Pacific journey at some point before 200 CE.

Since few healthy communities could survive the withering onslaught of starvation-based complexes, it didn't take long for state societies to conquer most of the world. With their concentrated focus on taking what doesn't belong to them, and on perfecting error-free methods and materials to do so, state societies were bound to enslave – or annihilate – each of their nonstate neighbors in turn. Even today, many if not most of the world's remaining nonstate societies are hiding out in places where state societies can't touch them: deep in jungles, high in mountains, or in other relatively inaccessible locations hard for starvation-culture peoples to reach. Either that, or they live in resource-poor areas not worth stealing.

Shafted

The word "shafted" is a mnemonic device you can use to remember the main characteristics of starvation culture (aka the state):

S Strongman rules
H Henchmen protect strongman
A Adults: "children" relying on strongman
F Fear of starvation: the motivation
T Thugs are admired
E Entertainment: watching sufferers
D Dregs and elites: society is divided into

S Strongman Rules

From the age-grade bully-leaders who dominated the starving Ik, to the emperors, dictators, presidents and prime ministers of state societies, all starvation-culture places tend to be run by the strongest males (or their female hangers-on). Indigenous societies on the other hand, have no strongman rulers.

H Henchmen Protect Strongman

From the "buddies" who backed up Ik bully-leaders, to the pampered people backing up North Korea's dictator Kim Jong Un, to the corporate overlords backing the American power elite, all starvation-culture leaders depend on henchmen to help them keep a stranglehold on their people.

A Adults Are Children Relying on Strongman

In starvation-culture societies most adults are enslaved to the strongman and his henchmen. Among the Ik, the elderly are little more than skeletons literally crawling along the ground, too weak from hunger and malnutrition to walk. The Ik people rely on their strongest males to carry government food back from the cities, but the men gobble up this food themselves, on the way home. In the early city-states almost everyone lived their lives in chains. Even in modern democracies most adults have little power over their government or even their own lives. Others dictate their purchasing power, the number of hours each year they must trade for this purchasing power, and the physical conditions they must endure to attain any such power. In many cases others even control when they are allowed to urinate and defecate.

Like children, state-society adults lack the skills necessary to work as teams to tackle their social problems, but must rely instead on their Strongman to sort these out. In contrast, adults in indigenous societies cooperate in groups to come to grips with community issues revolving around food, safety and spats between neighbors.

F Fear of Starvation Is the Motivator

Among the Ik, fear of death by starvation drove people to a maddening obsession with food – with eating food, watching for food, hunting for food, stealing food, gorging on food, fighting for food, and literally plucking food out of the mouths of anyone too weak to resist the insulting maneuver. In state societies, the deep-set fear that "enough is never enough" lingers in subterranean parts of the brain, motivating much of what we do on a day-to-day basis. Like the Ik, we are morbidly obsessed with the media we use to purchase food: money, gold, silver, stocks, bonds, etc. Even when we have hundreds of times more than we could ever spend, many of us are driven to distraction with the need to glom onto even more. And then more than that.

T Thugs Are Admired

The man the Ik admired most was the man who could filch the most from others. Anthropologist Colin Turnbull witnessed the following: Ik men still strong enough to stand on two feet shuffled to the nearest city to pick up government food for their starving families. On the trail back to their village, however, all but one of these men dove into the bushes beside the trail and gorged themselves on the food, leaving none of it for their "loved" ones back home. The only man who resisted gobbling up the food meant for his wife, was ridiculed to shreds by his companions.

The same admiration for thugs, thieves and con men shines like the sun in state societies. Thugs and thieves are often cast as the heroes of American movies. One such movie, "The Sting," starring famed actors Paul Newman and Robert Redford, won seven Academy Awards (in 1974). Other movies pushing con men as heroes: "Catch Me If You Can," "A Fish Called Wanda," "Paper Moon," "The Usual Suspects," "The Hustler," "American Hustle," "Matchstick Man," "Dirty Rotten Scoundrels," "The Wolf of Wall Street," and "White Men Can't Jump."

E Entertainment Is Watching Sufferers

Remember Lokol, the pre-adolescent Ik boy whose stomach was so distended by a bowel blockage that he was unable to sit, stand, or even lie down? Until he finally died, Lokol suffered through nights and days both by balancing himself on his ten-year-old hands and knees. His father, who considered his son's anguish one of the funniest things he'd ever seen, thought the neighbors might get a kick out of it too. So he invited them all over to gawk at the boy.

Like the Ik, members of state societies too seem often to get high on watching others suffer. Popular sports include football and hockey, in which players are maimed, break bones, and even die. In dog and cock fights, animals are fought to their deaths. Although not so common now, in the recent past comedy often involved people getting punched in the face, taking a fall, or otherwise getting beaten up – think Laurel and Hardy, or The Three Stooges, for example.

D Dregs or Elite: You're Either One or the Other

The Ik were split up into the strongest males on the one hand (the "elite"), and everyone else on the other (the "dregs"). While the strongest men ate, almost everyone else starved. A similar situation attains in all starvation-culture/state societies: most people are the dregs, or less-fortunates, while a handful make up the elite – those who will be able to afford to fly to other planets when the earth becomes uninhabitable and the dregs are left to die painful deaths. Americans too suffer under a class system; it's only a myth that they don't. In indigenous societies on the other hand, everyone's relatively equal; all get roughly the same healthy doses of food, shelter, medical care – and respect.

Are State Societies Really All That Bad?

Not everyone considers states bad hombres, of course, and states without a doubt provide some advantages over simpler kinds of societies. In a 2015 issue of *The Scandinavian Journal of Economics* James Ang lists some of the perks of living in a country, or state: "Well-functioning states provide welfare and security for their citizens, set up mechanisms for the exchange of goods and services, establish order in their societies, and have the capacity to improve economic outcomes" (Ang, 2015: 1134). What's more, most of the medicine and health-care procedures developed by modern state societies are marvels to behold – perks that few of us would choose to forego.

Not all states/countries, however, are "well-functioning." In fact, some have functioned so wretchedly that their people have risen up in revolt, toppling the existing power elite – after which another, new elite rises up to take its place.

Those that do function reasonably well obviously offer several shiny, valuable fringe benefits. But at what cost? "It's hard to imagine... primitives giving up their physical freedom, their varied diet, their egalitarian social structure, their relative freedom from famine, large-scale state wars, taxes and systematic subordination" to enjoy none of the above in state society (Scott, 2013). We in western state societies are not starving for food like our ancient ancestors were, but we are, nevertheless, starving for physical freedom, personal respect (the kind bestowed on everyone in egalitarian societies), and freedom from constant crime, violence and warfare.

Chapter 13

How Pinker and Diamond Screwed Up

Before waltzing back to the present – which we'll do in the final three chapters of this book – I want to climb into the ring with two wildly popular authors who contradict a chunk of what I've written here. In 2012, Harvard psychologist Stephen Pinker and UCLA geographer Jared Diamond published best sellers *The Better Angels of Our Nature,* and *The World Until Yesterday.* In the first, Pinker claims humans have gone from being raging monsters to tame little pussy cats today. In the second, Diamond claims that indigenous people are all brutal savages, and our pre-state ancestors were too. Through time Diamond has often switched careers – from physiology, to ornithology, to ecology and environmental history, and, finally, to geography, which he currently teaches at the University of California, Los Angeles.

If you haven't read these books and know zip about them, feel free to skip this section.

Stephen Pinker, Cherry-Picker

According to Pinker, before state societies popped up on the scene, we humans were virtual knuckle-draggers, violent King-Kong-types. Pinker "knows" that nonstate hunter-gatherers are more violent than state citizens, and that past state societies were more violent than modern ones. Throughout time it's been a bright and shiny straight line, says Pinker, from constant warfare, out-of-sight war casualties, and women roughed up 24/7, to today, with no world wars, far fewer war deaths, and far less beating up of women, children and people of color. Humans are naturally violent, opines Pinker. However, over time we've tamed our King-Kong nature – by sharpening our reasoning skills, our self-control, and our empathy.

According to most anthropologists and archaeologists – the experts trained to write the book, Pinker was not – none of this is true. The experts are quick to point out one of Pinker's main failings: cherry-picking. About *Better Angels*, University of Illinois historian Mark Micale writes, "Throughout this very long book [739 pages – not counting references and index], the author cherry-picked examples to advance his thesis; alternately idealized and stigmatized entire past eras; and continually dismissed masses of counterevidence" (Micale, 2018). Pinker cherry-picked facts about hunter-gatherers, horticulturalists, states, warfare, and large segments of human history.

You can almost imagine Stephen Picker... er, Pinker... spending much of his day on a ladder, head poked up in a cherry tree plucking the ripe, rosy little fruits off limbs and twigs and plopping them into his academic shoulder bag. Pinker's book is a collection of cherry-facts, each hand-picked by Pinker to prove his ill-gotten notion that humans, through time, have become increasingly angelic. In Pinker's mind, it's been a straight line from our brutish cave-dwelling ancestors down to the perfect twenty-first-century end product: a rosy-cheeked and perfectly tamed Mr. Pinker perched behind his oversized solid oak desk in his professorial office at Harvard, innocently and non-violently building collections of little non-facts, which he sends to an unsuspecting publisher to disseminate to an over-trusting public.

How Pinker Butchers Prehistory

To begin, Pinker doesn't seem to understand what the word "prehistory" means. It's very simple, Mr. Pinker: "prehistory" is history before the invention of writing. Now it's true that some people didn't have a way of writing down their history until recently – most hunter-gatherers, for example. Nevertheless, historians don't consider modern hunter-gatherers part of human prehistory. Mr. Pinker, however, does. He considers all of the simpler societies, like the Semai, Inuit, !Kung and so forth, "prehistoric."

What's more, when opining about prehistory, Mr. Pinker seems never to have heard of one of the major prehistoric time periods: the Neolithic. Spanning thousands of years, the Neolithic ushered in an extremely peaceful time period, one during which we stopped chasing wild game as it swept from one green pasture to the next, and edible wild plants as they ripened in one area and withered in others. No one pretending the Neolithic didn't exist can write intelligently about the sweep of human history. It just isn't possible.

Linda Fibiger, Senior Lecturer in Human Osteoarchaeology at the University of Edinburgh (she studies old bones), can't imagine how Pinker could be so dense as to shuffle the entire Neolithic off into a dark corner. Actually, she hints he might have been not dense but dodgy: "The omission of the Neolithic from Pinker's skeletal data set, even though this period marks one of the most profound subsistence and cultural changes in human history, is puzzling and unsettling... It may be explained through ignorance of this data source, *which seems unlikely*" (Fibiger, 2018) [emphasis my own].

Another of Pinker's astonishing claims is that throughout our eons-long prehistoric past we humans were at war nonstop, and that warfare regularly snuffed out the lives of a full quarter of all adult males. We're talking one out of every four men! The widely respected archaeologist Brian R. Ferguson says this is pure hogwash: "...this 'fact' – as widely invoked as it is – is utterly without empirical foundation... The axiom is a *myth*" (Ferguson, 2013b: 116)(emphasis Ferguson's, not mine).

Pinker's claim of extreme prehistoric violence relies heavily on one of his 114 figures, "Figure 2-2." Figure 2-2 is actually a bar graph titled "Percentage of Deaths in Warfare in Nonstate and State Societies." To dredge up this graph Pinker cherry-picked 22 archaeological sites of prehistoric skeletal remains that he says show extreme numbers of men killed in warfare. But Brian Ferguson says Pinker's list of 22 examples "...consists of cherry-picked cases... clearly unrepresentative of prehistory in general" (Ferguson, 2013b: 116).

The two most violent examples in Figure 2-2 are "Crow Creek" in South Dakota, dated 1325 CE, and "Nubia Site 117" along the Nile in Africa, dated 12,000–10,000 BCE. The oldest comes from a place called "Gobero" in Niger dated 14,000–6200 BCE, and the most recent is "2 sites in central California," 240–1770 CE.

Also plopped down on Pinker's Figure 2-2 are eight state-society examples – cherry-picked with a vengeance and supposedly representative of all the thousands of state societies that have lived and died on Planet Earth over the past 6000 years:

1. Ancient Mexico
2. All twentieth-century states
3. Twentieth-century European states
4. Seventeenth-century European states
5. Twentieth-century Europe and US
6. US in 2005 (war deaths)
7. The world in 2005 (battle deaths); and
8. The world in the twentieth century (wars and genocides)

Excuse me, Mr. Pinker. Any particular reason the most vicious and violent states failed to make your list? Um, like those from ancient Mesopotamia, ancient Egypt, China, Japan and India? Also, why do all your states but one hail from Europe or North America? As one scholar puts it, "Pinker's work exhibits an overly Western outlook. 'The West and the rest' is a mentality much on display in his pages" (Micale, 2018). Last time I checked, serving up claims about humanity based on two tiny parts of the human space-time continuum just doesn't fly with people in the know.

Flattened by the Experts

Scientists from disciplines Pinker ransacks for cherry-picked data have peeled Pinker like a ripe banana. For example, in one brief but concise paper titled "Pinker's List: Exaggerating Prehistoric War Mortality," Brian Ferguson skewers Pinker's entire thesis. Ferguson takes each of Pinker's 22 nonstate examples and shows why Pinker's analysis is full of holes big enough to steer a cow through.

Right off the bat Ferguson knocks seven of Pinker's 22 bony archaeological sites off the list, since they show no war deaths whatsoever – with one showing no deaths whatsoever, from war or anything else (Ferguson, 2013b: 116). Most of the remaining 15 sites are indeed examples of large numbers of people dying violent deaths – but are totally atypical of prehistoric sites in general ("Indian Knoll, then, is not representative or typical of prehistoric violence..."; "Crow Creek and Norris Farms are... extreme in their levels of violence..." (Ferguson, 2013b: 121; 125)).

What does Ferguson say about the four sites mentioned earlier – Crow Creek, Nubia Site 117, Gobero and the two sites in central California? Here's his take on each:

1. "Crow Creek" – Atypical

The human bones from Crow Creek were buried during a period of horrific drought, with epic dry spells lasting 40–60 years at a time. Skeletons show "clear signs of nutritional stress." In lieu of starving to death, people presumably fought neighbors to the death over the last scraps of food. Although at Crow Creek a whopping 486 people died simultaneously, this level of violence is highly atypical for prehistoric communities – even for this generally violent time and place.

2. "Nubia Site 117" – Atypical

At Nubia Site 117 archaeologists uncovered the bones of 59 ancient humans, some of whom definitely died violently (they were buried with honest-to-gosh stone points chucked into their bones). But how many died violently? Although Pinker says half, one in ten is more likely. What's more, some archaeologists think the graveyard these 59 were buried in might have been specially set aside for those who died violent deaths, since just across the Nile a similar cemetery holds 39 people, only one a victim of violence. The main point about Nubia Site 117, however, is this: it is not typical of prehistoric violence. It is "unique in the world for [its] combination of antiquity and carnage" (Ferguson, 2013b: 117–18).

3. "Gobero" – No violence

Buried at Gobero were 200 ancient people dug up out of several lakeside cemeteries – none of whom showed signs of violent deaths. This was one of the seven sites Ferguson scratched off Pinker's list right from the get-go. Why in the world Pinker included it and the other six scratched off by Ferguson is a mystery. Carelessness? The result of writing about a subject he knew little about? A dishonest attempt to pad his results?

4. "2 sites in central California" – Atypical

Central California has "long been recognized for exceptional rates of violence among prehistoric peoples." In other words, its prehistoric archaeological sites, like dwarves and albinos, stand far outside the norm.

At the end of his takedown of Pinker, Ferguson notes that "War does not go forever backwards in time. It had a beginning. We are not hard-wired for war. We learn it." To see war, says Ferguson, societies need to get large, snooty (hierarchal), complex, and more like couch potatoes (settling down in one place rather than chasing edible wild plants and animals all over the place) (Ferguson, 2013b: 126; 116). In other words, war is far more a feature of states than of nonstates.

Butchering History

Pinker cherry-picks prehistory, but doesn't stop there. He cherry-picks history as well. At the Ohio State University, prehistorian Randolph Roth says Pinker doesn't know his history. Real historians, says Roth, don't see a decline in human violence at all: "Pinker's defense is flawed... [T]he data gathered by historians do not show long-term declines in individual or collective violence" (Roth, 2018). Roth also takes a jab at Pinker's background – psychology – suggesting that other backgrounds might be better for writing a book about historical violence, disciplines like primatology, neurology or endocrinology. Personally, I would add history and archaeology to the list.

Another historian, Harvard's Daniel Lord Smail, chides Pinker for butchering the Middle Ages: "Pinker's depiction of violence in medieval Europe... includes serious misrepresentations... [and] his handling of the scholarship... raises doubts about his treatment of other periods" (Smail, 2018). For medieval violence, Pinker points to Anne Boleyn's beheading by Henry VIII, Elizabeth I's torture chambers, and violent German fairy tales. But ISIS today beheads people, George W. Bush kept torture chambers, and modern movies for teens can out-grisly the Grimms any day of the year.

Pinker is an equal-opportunity butcher. It's not just the past that he butchers but the present as well. For example, he utters not one peep about:

- violence related to imperialism
- violence related to the slicing and dicing of indigenous peoples
- violence related to the "criminal hacking of government computer systems"
- violence real and potential related to human-caused climate change
- violence real and potential related to nuclear weapons

(Micale, 2018)

Jared Diamond's (Dead-in-the-Water) Hypothesis

According to Jared Diamond, in the game of life states are the big winners, nonstates the losers. Take any state society, he says, and you'll find life safer and sweeter there than in any indigenous society – past or present. States according to Diamond are the cat's pajamas, and, a la Hobbs, life in nonstates is nasty, brutish and short.

Diamond is wrong. It's not states but untouched nonstates that are the world's superstars. Soon after it was born, the state began beating up on nonstates, but before that the nonstate was the proverbial Garden of Eden. After 4000 BCE, nonstates living in the shadow of a state had two choices: (1) morph into fierce people who could survive the pummeling the states regularly visited upon their heads, or (2) hightail it to harsher parts of the globe – parts that states wouldn't want to trek to or snatch up for their own selfish purposes.

For most of the past 6000 years, states forced swarms of slaves to do their dirty work. Even if nearby hunter-gatherers and horticulturalists weren't sitting on lands dotted with deposits of gold, iron or other coveted minerals – lands the states salivated over until they could rip them away for themselves – the states could still mine their nonstate neighbors for slaves. Over the years, in other words, states have shattered all nonstate societies into mere shadows of their former selves. Even our beautiful Semai, Mbuti, !Kung and Inuit would be healthier if they could survive outside areas where it's difficult to secure food and other life necessities.

Diamond's notion that all nonstates are "nasty, brutish and short" is based on negligent scholarship. After dumping all modern hunter-gatherer and horticultural groups into a single bag, he gingerly lifts out only the nasty, brutish ones, holds them up, and says, "See? This is the what all nonstates are like."

In short, like Pinker, Diamond too is a cherry-picker. He leaves peaceful, pleasant groups like the Semai, Mbuti and Hopi hidden deep in his bag, hoping we won't peek in and see how relatively idyllic they are. The Semai certainly don't suffer lives that are nasty, brutish and short. Nor do the Mbuti, Hopi, or any number of other modern hunter-gatherers and horticulturalists.

Nasty indigenous peoples have become nasty in order to survive the treachery of nearby state societies. "Contemporary foraging societies, far from being untouched examples of our deep past, are up to their necks in the 'civilised world,'" says Yale anthropologist James C. Scott. In a feeble attempt to bolster his bogus theory, Diamond pulls 36 indigenous people out of his bag, and except for the people of Highland New Guinea "all of the other 35 societies... for the last five thousand years, have been deeply involved in a world of trade, states and empires..." (Scott, 2013).

The South American Yanomamo and Siriono, for example, two of Diamond's "nasty 36," were horticulturalists originally. Then the state moved in – in the form of Spanish settlers and conquistadores – and life changed forever for the Yanomamo and Siriono. The Spanish forced both groups into slavery – those at least who survived the crippling diseases the Spanish toted over from the Old World. About these two groups Scott says, "Like almost all the groups Diamond considers, they have been trading with outside kingdoms and states (and raiding them) for much of the past three thousand years; their beliefs and practices have been shaped by contact, trade goods, travel and intermarriage" (Scott, 2013).

Over the centuries, those Yanomamo and Siriono who escaped deadly Spanish diseases and slave-catchers, slinked off into the jungle and turned to hunting and foraging to survive. I don't know about you, but if someone killed most of my family and friends and then ripped away my land, I might become nasty too.

So, contrary to what Diamond and Pinker want us to believe, modern indigenous groups are not "...museum exhibits of the way life was lived for the entirety of human history 'until yesterday' – preserved in amber for our examination" (Scott,

2013). Before states sliced, diced and skewered them, our indigenous ancestors apparently lived like Adam and Eve in the Garden of Eden. As noted in the previous section about Stephen Pinker and in other sections of this book, the archaeological record forks over much support for the notion that human life pre-state was close to idyllic.

Even the "nasty and brutish" nonstates Diamond pulls out of his bag are in several respects superior to any state society. As argued previously, "It's hard to imagine Diamond's primitives giving up their physical freedom, their varied diet, their egalitarian social structure, their relative freedom from famine, large-scale state wars, taxes and systematic subordination in exchange for what Diamond imagines to be 'the king's peace'" (Scott, 2013).

By "the king's peace" Diamond is essentially referring to the violent police units held in check on side benches by all state societies, units just waiting for their chance to blister any and all wrongdoers they can catch in the act of wrongdoing. Diamond erroneously assumes that the king's peace is necessary to tame our supposed inherent violent human nature. But humans aren't inherently violent. Naturally we're likely to snap, crackle and pop if we're treated inhumanely (by, say, states), but that doesn't mean we're naturally violent. In other words, states are the source of the problem Diamond supposes they're designed to fix.

In short, both Pinker and Diamond are wrong. Before the state reared its ugly head life was good. The state is an artificial, anti-human bogeyman forced upon humanity against its will, kept alive by starvation culture – a set of values and beliefs constantly whispering in your third ear, "you'll never have enough of what you need." The state relies on your willingness to fork over your personal power to a small elite, an elite who also believe they'll never have enough, that starvation lurks forever, like a savage, snarling beast, around all corners.

Chapter 14

Still Starving After All These Years

ISIL and Modern Climate Change

Are we living through the beginning stages of the same kind of horrendous disaster the world's earliest farmers suffered in 4000 BCE? In some ways what happened in Mesopotamia is strikingly similar to certain current events. As in 4000 BCE the world today is experiencing rapid climate change. In both time periods this sudden atmospheric change was followed by the rise of crude human violence: in 4000 BCE starvation culture was born, and today Islamic jihadi groups not averse to horrifying behavior such as public beheadings, have become a major problem worldwide.

Midway through 2019 the United Nations warned that "a half billion people already live in places turning into desert, and soil is being lost between 10 and 100 times faster than it is forming..." (Flavelle, 2019). A major consequence: people are flooding to the borders of the wealthier parts of the world, pressing their noses up against the window panes of those borders, hunger in their eyes. Alternately, they are storming those borders, shoving their way in and demanding food, water and shelter. Shades of 4000 BCE, when starvation-culture peoples overcame the wealthy, peaceful peoples living the good life at the Tigris and Euphrates. "People don't stay and die where they are. People migrate," said Pete Smith, professor of plant and soil science at Scotland's University of Aberdeen (Flavelle, 2019).

Over the five-year period from 2010 to 2015 the number of people flocking to the US border from El Salvador, Honduras and Guatemala increased fivefold; during that same time "a dry period that left many with not enough food... was so unusual that scientists suggested it bears the signal of climate change...

'You're sort of reaching a breaking point with land itself and its ability to grow food and sustain us,' said Aditi Sen, a senior policy adviser on climate change at Oxfam America..." (Flavelle, 2019).

Islamic radicalism too has reared its ugly head at least in part due to climate change. Drought in the Middle East has led to water and food shortages, to a lack of employment, and to deep-seated fear and anger. In Iraq – the original home of starvation culture – the Islamic State is recruiting more members from drought-stricken areas than from elsewhere in the country: "Around Tikrit, Saddam Hussein's northern Iraqi hometown, ISIL appears to have attracted much more support from water-deprived communities than from their better-resourced peers" (Schwartzstein, 2017).

As their rain and rivers disappeared, twenty-first-century Iraqi farmers turned to wells to water their crops and flocks. But in many cases, these too have run dry. "After several years of energetic groundwater extraction near the oil refining town of Baiji, Samir Saed's two wells ran dry in early 2014, forcing him to lay off the two young men he employed as farm laborers. Jobless and angry, he suspects they soon joined ISIL" (Schwartzstein, 2017).

By 2012, half of Iraq's farmers lacked safe drinking water, and in 2012–13, tens of thousands abandoned their land and moved to city slums. Speaking about ISIL, Abbas Luay Essawi, a herder from Hawija said, "They just watched us. We were like food on the table to them." Jabouri, the tribal sheikh from Shirqat said, "ISIL is gone for now, but with all these water and heat problems, things will only get worse. We need help now" (Schwartzstein, 2017).

The problem isn't restricted to Iraq. In 2011 the drought that hit Somalia was also linked to climate change. That same year the jihadi group Al-Shabaab responded with "water weaponization" – cutting water supplies off to cities that refused to support them. This and a lack of aid coming in from outside Somalia (Al-Shabaab clipped that off too) led to the deaths of more than one quarter million people (Werrell and Femia, 2019).

The violent groups in both time periods are/were determined to conquer groups more complex than they are. Both use/used tactics too abhorrent for their advanced target groups to use in return: in 4000 BCE this was the use of weapons against human beings, something the complex groups at that time found as shocking and disturbing as we today find beheadings and suicide bombings. In other words, each culturally advanced target group, both today and in the past, was handicapped by its humanitarian sensitivities.

So, in a few highly significant ways we're living through a situation similar to the one fifth-millenium BCE Mesopotamians suffered. In other ways, however, the parallels are a mirage. First, starvation culture in 4000 BCE was primitive down to the bone, while their Smart-People victims were more advanced socially than most people are in the world today – more egalitarian, more peaceful, and more mentally and physically healthy. In comparison with Alpha's 4000 BCE desert rats, today's jihadists hail from relatively sophisticated cultures, while the rest of us, when it comes to quality of life at least, fall somewhere between our modern jihadists and the 4000-BCE Smart People.

Second, although our stomachs churn at the thought of jihadi beheadings and suicide bombings, our own Western leaders use torture techniques that most of us find almost as horrifying. The fact is, although we've each developed our own distinctive brand of it, both Westerners and jihadists alike are inheritors of starvation culture. A look back at this book's first chapter will disabuse you of the notion that Westerners, and particularly Americans, live in anything but starvation-culture societies.

Apocalypse Now?

By the end of this century or the next, most humans could very well be wiped off the face of the earth. How and why? Although my money's on climate change, it's hard to say which aspect of climate could be the final cause of a possible collapse. Will it be oscillations of heat/cold and wet/dry too extreme for us to handle? Or will it be methane "burps" from oceans, tundras and ice caps, burps large enough to set fire to the planet?

Or maybe "nuclear winter" will rob us of sunlight, uncontaminated soil and water clean enough for growing food. If militant Islamists or other rogue groups get their hands on nuclear material and the means to control it, we're in for trouble. Meanwhile North Korea's nuclear program is under the control of a man seemingly under the spell of mental-health abnormalities.

I don't think the end will result from runaway viruses, since the human group has always included individuals immune to any virus that we as a species have faced in the past. If even a handful of individuals in the simpler societies escape a worldwide viral epidemic we should be okay – i.e., the species would probably survive. I have little hope the state societies will survive, including most inhabitants of North America, Europe, Australia, and the industrialized parts of Asia. I doubt that the tropics, the lands north and south of the Equator, will be cool enough to support life, including animal, plant or human.

Although the purpose of this book is not to spell out ways for humans to avoid an apocalypse, it might nevertheless provide a roadmap for those who survive such a catastrophe. Once they've gotten back on their feet again and can worry about more than finding food and water to survive in a bombed- or burnt-out world, this book might provide those people with ideas about how to avoid making the same mistakes we made in the twentieth and twenty-first centuries (and of course well before that, since the cause of the apocalypse began six millennia ago, in the Middle East, after 4000 BCE). In other words this book can be seen as a survivor's manual. It might help some small group begin the human family all over again, and give it a fresh start with none of the baggage we've had to struggle with for the past several millennia.

On the other hand, humanity might just find a way out of the blind alleys we've boxed ourselves into. Then what? Many of us believe that one day, if we try hard enough, we'll put an end to war, poverty and all our other sociocultural ugliness. We believe that the only reasons we haven't scotched these ills to date is because (1) we just haven't tried hard enough, (2) haven't convinced enough of our fellow citizens to follow our lead, or (3) haven't come up with the precise magical formula that will get the job done. And yet humanity has been trying to pluck out its ugly chin hairs for millennia now, and what do we have to show for it? Not much: a few democracies dotting the globe, many of them struggling to stay afloat; better health for some; and a train load of technological marvels that some get to enjoy, others not so much.

Where We Are Today (In Poor Shape and in the Dark)

Despite this mixed bag of happy advancements, most of humanity lives under the gloomy cloud of potential warfare, including nuclear war. And even in the healthiest democracies a small, power elite holds almost absolute sway over We the People. Oh sure, occasionally this elite lets us think we have the upper hand, because when they don't, we make life difficult for them for a while. They then attempt to look contrite and hand us back a bit of our power. Next, they roll out their shiny propaganda machines and con a majority of us into thinking (erroneously) that we hold massive amounts of power over them.

The last time the elite in America totally forgot to play the contrition game was during the "Age of the Robber Barons," in the late 1800s and the early 1900s. During the Age of the Robber Barons, several big industrialists lied and cheated their way into great riches and gilded mansions. After they took control of Congress, Congress did their bidding over the bidding of the people. Then the Great Depression happened, and Franklin Delano Roosevelt managed to convince his wealthy brethren that they'd overstepped their bounds. For several decades after that, America's uber wealthy retreated, played dead, and let us think they didn't hold almost absolute power over us.

But the power elite can't play dead for long; they have short memories (and, in America, no great relationship with the historical record). So now, early in the twenty-first century, they're at it again, stomping all over the rest of us. In the US the gap between rich and poor is now set to be wider than in any other country in the world:

> The proposed tax reform package [of Dec., 2017] stakes out America's bid to become *the most unequal society in the world* [my italics], and will greatly increase the already high levels of wealth and income inequality between the richest 1% and the poorest 50% of Americans. (Alston, 2017)

In non-democratic state societies, of course, the plight of the poor is even worse. In non-democracies, the power elite abuse the People to their hearts' content. When this abuse leads to citizens literally starving to death, the result is peoples' revolts: in Russia, China, Spain, Cuba and elsewhere. *What do we have to lose?* people say. *We're going to die either way.* Many do die, on both sides, and then the power elite gains the upper hand again – led by Stalin in Russia, Franco in Spain, Mao in China, Castro in Cuba, and so on.

Sorry to Say It, But Things Are Getting Worse, Not Better

On some level, you've accepted the "fact" that to be ruled over by humans who don't have your best interests at heart is as normal as breathing. You've even accepted that you don't have the right to perch on any portion of land unless the power elite give you permission to do so. If you can't afford to buy land from a bank, you are forced to fork over your hard-earned money to someone who can, and then they'll let you squat on their land. Otherwise, inside your state-style society you are forbidden to spend any more than X amount of time on any land anywhere.

Camp out in a public park? You're a squatter, and pitched into jail. Sleep in the woods? The owner of the woods calls the cops to drive you out. Set up tents, with others, behind a Big Box store? In no time flat the store owners are on the phone to law enforcement. And not only do the local police tear down your tents, they also walk away with all your belongings.

Although you've been brainwashed to believe the above is normal and natural, it isn't. A quick glance through the laws of nature reveals no law whatsoever giving a few humans all rights over the ground all the other millions of us need to walk on. No Semai individual owns any part of the forest all Semais live in. Same with the Inuit, same with Native Americans, and same with indigenous people in general. In the late 1700s a Native American named Turk, a Wyandot, admonished the white settlers who were suddenly flooding into his homeland in the old American Northwest Territory, carving out little pieces of it which they claimed were theirs and theirs alone. Turk said to them, "No one in particular can justly claim this [land]; it belongs in common to us all; no earthly being has an exclusive right to it. The Great Spirit above is the true and only owner of this soil; and He has given us all an equal right to it" (McCullough, 2019).

In the past, even the British recognized the truth of Turk's words. According to ancient Teutonic law, all the people of Great Britain owned the land in common. Later, when the feudal system gave some of the land to little "lords" (little earthly "gods"), their serfs still had free use of vast common lands – which they could use to hunt and gather food and fuel.

But then – as we all know from watching old TV reruns

of "Robin Hood" – the wily old land "gods" ripped even the common lands out of the hands of the masses. Here's how and why that happened: When in the 1500s the West became hungry for wool – to be fashioned into clothing and other items – it began to pay handsome sums to whomever would supply them with large quantities of it (i.e., wool). So in part, this monumental land grab happened because human land gods realized that the land their insignificant little farmers were using to produce their bread and butter, could make them, the land gods, as flush as King Tut – if they ripped that land away from the farmers and plopped sheep on it.

And that, my friends, was the end of common land in Britain, i.e., land shared by all and all alike the way the earth's remaining healthy societies share it. What came after this gigantic land grab was even uglier. After getting bumped off their land – land they'd used for centuries to feed themselves and their children – many Brits had to resort to roaming the countryside, scrounging for food wherever they could find it. A lot of vagabonding and begging began going on. Then the lords realized they'd made a mistake booting their feudal tenants off their land, because they needed those bodies to do all the sheep-work that they themselves didn't want to do (and couldn't do even if they'd wanted to – there was just too much of it).

And it wasn't only the land grabbers who needed labor. The guys who bought the wool needed lots of hands, heads and strong backs too – to card, clean, spin, weave, sew and market the wool, to build thousands of looms, sheep shears, shearing sheds, and wagons to carry the wool, drivers to drive wool and wool products to market, accountants to keep records and prep tax returns, and so forth. In short, the need for new kinds of labor was gargantuan.

So, the wily British land gods began passing laws making it a punishable crime to vagabond or beg for food. After that, you either spent your life locked up or working as a wage slave for land pigs, for wool industrialists, or for some other kind of industrialist or business owner – usually for a pauper's pittance. What's more, no longer could you park your carcass for more than a few days at a time on any part of Britain's land mass, since all of the land was now locked up by land lords.

In 1530, during the reign of Henry the VIII, "Beggars old and unable to work receive a beggar's license. On the other hand, whipping and imprisonment for sturdy vagabonds [sic]. They are to be tied to the cart-tail and whipped until the blood streams... then to swear an oath to go back to their birthplace or to where they have lived the last three years and to 'put themselves to labor.'" Later it got worse: the second time you were found failing to offer yourself up as a wage slave, it was off with an ear, and for the third, execution "as a hardened criminal and enemy of the common weal" (Marx, 2012).

Land grabbing and displacement of farmers continues to this day. Just as the state did in the UK in the 1500s, so it is doing in other parts of the world today. In India, for example, Pranab Katni Basu outlines the dastardly process as it unfolds in the twenty-first-century: global elites choose an area of India they want to barge into, and India boots the farmers out of that area. These areas are called "special economic zones," or SEZs, and if you manage to get your greedy little global-capital hands on an Indian SEZ, you will be showered with affection: no need to pay customs duties, income taxes, excise taxes, water bills, or electric bills! India will pay those for you! And – icing on the cake – no need to endure those pesky, irritating little things called "labor unions," because the Indian state will deny its own people the right to stand together to beat back any of the injustices starvation culture likes to drop on the heads of salaried workers.

In West Bengal a group of vultures wants to rip prime agricultural land away from Indians who have farmed it for generations. These industrialists are hot to build a car-manufacturing plant on an area of super-rich food-growing land, and violence is being used to force the farmers off it. But the way of life of these farmers revolves around farming the land, and they don't care how much money the state gives them – losing the land means the death of their culture. To them, this is inconceivable. No matter that in West Bengal it's against the law to change multi-crop land into non-agricultural land, the government is plowing ahead anyway with stripping these farmers of their reason for living – their land (Basu, 2007).

How do we put the kibosh on the state? I have a few ideas. If you're interested, read on.

Chapter 15

The Fix: Erasing Starvation Culture

Here, Have Some Free Money (The Need for a Universal Basic Income)

Remember: at the heart of starvation culture is our deep subconscious fear that enough is never enough. The behaviors of hoarders, people with food disorders, billionaires and millionaires who keep working well past retirement age – all of these are probable outward manifestations of this fear. But in one way this fear may be a good thing, since it might provide a key to reversing starvation culture aka the state. If we can get people to the point where they know deep in the mammalian part of their brains that they needn't worry about food, clothing, shelter, medical care or any other of life's necessities, there's a chance this fear will melt away – or at least level off.

But how would we relax our mammalian brains to this degree? One possibility: through a universal basic income, or UBI. Under a UBI system, every citizen would receive free money, without having to work a job, or jump through hoops to get it: "Universal Basic Income (UBI) can be described as a form of unconditional transfer payment to the entirety of the populace, without means testing or work requirements" (Chohan, 2017).

"Pie-in-the-sky ideas," you might be thinking. "No one's going to bite on that one." Actually, as the gap between rich and poor has yawned deeper and wider over the past few decades, the UBI has become an increasingly popular idea. The universal basic income is "becoming an ever more appealing idea in the twenty-first century" and "is no longer considered a 'crackpot idea of the radical left'" (Chohan, 2017). The UBI is being touted as a lifeboat guaranteeing that even though the future might bring a shortage of paying jobs, everyone's basic needs would nevertheless be met.

Because the universal basic income is being taken seriously at the moment, I believe it should be tagged as one of the main preliminary focuses of those of us interested in replacing starvation culture and the state. In the second half of the nineteenth century, Susan B. Anthony desperately wanted to win a smorgasbord of rights for American women, but she was smart enough to throw her energy behind one and one only: the right to vote. Through the vote, she reasoned, women would win their other rights, but without the vote, other rights would be hard to snag. So, for decades Anthony campaigned tirelessly to enfranchise women, encouraging other women too to concentrate first and foremost on women's suffrage. And although she died before reaching her goal, it was only 14 years after her death that the Nineteenth Amendment to the US Constitution was passed, giving American women at last the right to step up to a ballot box and cast their votes in American elections.

Do we need a twenty-first-century Susan B. Anthony to fight for the UBI? Yes! With a guaranteed income, citizens of state societies would acquire the time and energy needed to fight for other rights humanity now lacks. No longer could the power elite force citizens to work for peanuts, or under conditions unfit for animals. Nor could they count on citizens to sign up to fight wars simply because they lack alternative means of satisfying basic needs. In short, guaranteeing an income to all is the first step in erasing the barbarity that is the state.

Child Rearing Is Key to Erasing the State

If starvation culture teaches us nothing else, it's that enculturation – child rearing methods – is the golden key to sociocultural change. Starvation culture arose in the first place simply because children in long-starving populations lost in gigantic, empty desertlands had nothing to emulate but the psychotic behaviors of the adults around them. Since 1776, the main purpose of the world's political revolutions has been to stamp out, or at least neutralize, starvation culture. But to a great extent, these revolutions, like damp sticks of dynamite, have fizzled out. And they fizzled out primarily because they failed to change their old state-drenched child-rearing practices.

During and after their 1917 revolution, Russians continued to teach their children starvation-culture ways. As a result, Russian children grew up knowing only broken ways to cope with their altered political situation. For example, starvation culture continued to teach them to fear and obey a power elite. And since it taught them they needed one strong father figure to bow and scrape to, that's exactly how the twentieth-century Russian and Chinese revolutions ended: with dictators Mao Tse Dung and Joseph Stalin grabbing each country by the throat and squeezing. And the 1930s civil war between the Spanish power elite and the Spanish people ended the same: with Francisco Franco, a harsh dictator who immediately pinned the country down in a stranglehold.

Starvation culture teaches us that our national leaders are scary fathers, almost god-like, with god-like magical powers, virtually impossible to overpower. Until it was torn down in 2016, the Chinese still bowed and scraped to a giant gold statue of Mao, as if Mao were a god on high. Chinese revolutionaries needed to teach their children – but did not – that leaders are simply ordinary people who put their pants on one leg at a time.

In contrast, most indigenous cultures do look at their leaders as ordinary people with skills in certain specific areas. To lead their seal hunts the Inuit choose seal hunting experts, to lead their bear hunts, bear hunting experts. The Inuit recognize no overarching father-god leader whose job it is to lead them generally in all matters. What's more Inuit leaders have no power over the Inuit people; a leader can be "fired" after only one afternoon of poor performance. The Inuit know that just like other normal, ordinary human beings, their leaders bleed when cut, and sometimes weep when things go wrong. What's more, all Inuit learn these important facts from their earliest awareness of the world around them.

Another way political revolutionaries fail to alter poisonous child-rearing practices circles around a major hallmark of starvation culture: violence. To erase the state, children must be taught to avoid falling back on violent behavior as a problem-solving tool. The state was born out of the fiery violence that allowed ancient starving people to survive. It was brute force that enabled at least a few Alphas to survive long enough to procreate – by stealing food out of the mouths of everyone else, and, when necessary, swinging clubs around and hitting everyone in the head until they handed over their edibles. Eventually the ideal person became the most skillful thief, violent or not. The result? Today starvation-culture people view violence as an acceptable way of solving problems – especially problems they consider otherwise insoluble.

Near the beginning of the French Revolution, Maximilien Robespierre (one of the Revolution's main leaders), was dead-set against using violence to quash any resistance to the cause. After all, the goal of this bloody war was to deep-six the violence France's power elite used to hobble French citizens. Eventually, however, Robespierre's starvation-culture upbringing kicked in, and he helped unleash one of the bloodiest episodes in France's long history, the "Reign of Terror." In less than a year, 17,000 "resisters" were executed, many guillotined, including even some of Robespierre's republican comrades. Another 10,000 died in prison (Silverstein, 2018).

Despite Robespierre's lunge into starvation-culture violence, the French Revolution eventually morphed into one of the more successful revolutions that have rocked the world over the past three centuries. As a thriving constitutional republic France today is governed by a president, and a parliament built of an upper and lower house. But to finally coast to a stop as a free republic took decades – from 1798 to the 1870s. Meanwhile, for over half a century France bounced back and forth between republic and monarchy. At first a Republic, it dissolved into a dictatorship under Napoleon, and finally, in 1870, after Napoleon's nephew was pitched out on his ear, a republic again. All of this gave French parents time to rear their children in new and improved ways, so that the culture eventually changed enough to support democratic values and institutions. In other words, the French began to raise children who grew up to demand liberty as their birthright.

To a great extent the American Revolution hit pay dirt because the colonists were part indigenous African and part American Indian – both culturally and genetically. As a result, their child-rearing practices were less steeped in starvation-culture sickness than they would have been otherwise. What's more, for over a century, Europe's state-society kings largely stayed out of America's hair, allowing it to "grow up" free of heavy-handed starvation-culture chains. In short, compared to those in Europe, American child-rearing practices were far less steeped in starvation-culture grunge.

Also, as discussed previously, the colonists patterned their new government in part along the lines of the Iroquois political system, giving the new United States, right from the start, a partly indigenous, non-starvation-culture government. However, as US native and indigenous-African influences have weakened over the past 200 years, so has the strength of the American republic. Almost all immigrants to America today hail from starvation-culture countries. And increasingly, immigrants to America come from the more highly starvation-culture-soaked areas of the world. In 1960 foreign-born residents of the US were distributed principally from democratic countries:

Italy 1,257,000
Germany 990,000

Canada 953,000
UK 833,000
Poland 748,000

But by 2000, the distribution was dramatically different: the majority of foreign-born residents in the US hailed from autocratic countries, or countries with poorly functioning democracies:

Mexico 7,841,000
China 1,391,000
Philippines 1,222,000
India 1,007,000
Cuba 952,000
(Chua, 2018)

In a nutshell, compared to what it was in 1776 American society today is far more starvation-based, and far less free. On the upside, however, some of our late-twentieth and twenty-first-century immigrants will return to their home countries glowing with a variety of democratic ideals under their belts. This migration of democratic values to non-democratic countries is vital to our cause, since to replace starvation culture and the state, we need to bring most of the world along with us. Otherwise the remaining states will be tempted to crush any budding new stateless societies. Of course democracy doesn't eliminate the state, but people in democracies do have a bit more freedom to jump from the ugliness of the state into something kinder.

And yet even in our most democratic republics – in modern Europe, North America, Australia and a few others – children are taught not how to live in true democracies, but in repressive starvation-culture states. From birth, for example, citizens are taught to bow to the will of alpha males and females. This begins in the cradle, with infants taught to bend to the will of parents, and after leaving home to the will of teachers. In contrast, among the Semai it is taboo to force children to do anything they don't want to do (unless, of course, they're about to hurt themselves or others). Finally, after leaving school, we're taught to bend to the will of employers. So we're socialized not to live in democracies, but in autocracies.

When they supported kibbutzniks in the early State of Israel, the Israelis had the right idea. The aim of the intellectuals who invented the kibbutz was to create an eventual utopia. In the early kibbutzim, children were raised not by their starvation-culture biological parents, but by specially trained "nannies" who taught small age-cohorts of children to work together, and to pooh-pooh social hierarchy. Kibbutzniks were all paid the same, no matter what kind of work they did, so children learned early a non-snobbish way of looking at the world.

However, as an influx of immigrants from starvation-based countries swept into Israel, the kibbutz began to falter. The newcomers started demanding that their children live at home fulltime rather than in the children's homes. They began pushing for higher wages for certain kinds of work, and this new emphasis on differential wages shot social hierarchy back into the mix. The result? Many if not most kibbutzim children were now being reared by starvation-culture adults teaching them the old starvation-culture ways. This, of course, threw a monkey wrench into everything. During the "kibbutz crisis" of the 1970s and '80s, kibbutz head-counts began falling like leaves in a brisk autumn wind.

At least one source claims it was kibbutz mothers who first insisted on raising their children at home. As more and more women from starvation-culture countries moved onto the kibbutzim, kibbutz women were increasingly drenched in the fear of "never having enough." In starvation-culture countries women try to quash this fear by raising sons who, after rising to the top of the social hierarchy, have the financial chops to protect their elderly parents. And since women usually outlive men, women are doubly in need of such financial help in their elder years.

I believe this is what incoming Israeli mothers wanted: to raise their own sons to be brighter and "better" than other sons, and so have a keener chance of grabbing onto one of the scarce seats in the inner circle of the power elite. Never mind that the early kibbutzim had no power elite; starvation-culture thinking is not eminently logical.

Mr Benayoun said the main reason for returning children to their parents was "pressure from the mothers. The children themselves said they wanted to be in the children's house." Mr Zohar, one of the founders of [the kibbutz] Baram 48 years ago, opposed the decision. Admitting that many parents wanted their children to sleep at home, he says: "Kids are not pets. You have to imagine what is best for the kids, not what is best for the parents" (Cockburn, 1997).

In sum, if a society aims to free itself from the ugly bonds of starvation culture it must do some first aid on its socialization methods. As did the early Israeli kibbutzim, it must begin to rear its children in new and different ways, ways that resemble the childrearing practices of the world's remaining non-violent, non-hierarchical societies such as the Semai, !Kung, Inuit and others. Like the Semai, it must allow children the freedom to do what they please – as long as they're not hurting themselves or others. And at very young ages children must be taught to live in groups of age cohorts, and to create a wide variety of consensus decisions within these cohorts. They must learn that it's the group that's king, not some individual god-like leader. Children must be taught non-violent games, and to abhor physical violence. The word "kibbutz" comes from the Hebrew word "qibbus," a gathering. If we could zap our daycare centers into "child-gathering homes" where children are taught from birth to live non-violently and non-snobbishly, and to make decisions consensually, we'd be well along the road to overcoming many of our societal sicknesses.

On top of suggesting new and important child-rearing techniques, the kibbutz also sends us a warning: for child centers to work, women must be able to count on financial security from sources other than their adult children. In addition, women will need goals other than motherhood to give their lives meaning. Not long ago one of my acquaintances said, "I haven't done a thing important in my life – except raise my wonderful, talented children." In a healthy, nonstate society women will need ways other than motherhood for making themselves feel good about who they are.

Peaceniks Are Not Cowards

In addition to new ways of child rearing another part of the Fix involves scotching our subconscious adulation of war and warriors. A while ago, an article in *The New Yorker* caught my eye. "They Die Young" was about a fictitious and peaceful Malaysian indigenous group, "the Pawong." Near the beginning of the article, the author's boyfriend, Glauber, is full of contempt for the Pawong:

> [T]he Pawong... don't understand war or even conflict at all. Neighboring tribes come and slaughter them and rape their women, and the Pawong don't know to defend themselves or retaliate. It doesn't even occur to them that they could respond... The Pawong... live in fear that their enemies will come back, but they don't prepare for it. They just dread it and dread it, and teach their children to dread it, and then, when their children are properly scared, it makes them incredibly proud... (Bordas, 2017)

The Pawong sound suspiciously like the Semai, discussed here and there throughout this book. Instead of flying off the handle when provoked, the Semai sweep deeper into the forest. To them quickstepping away to avoid violence is as admirable as waltzing off to war is to us. Far from considering it cowardice, they consider it supreme intelligence. This is a good example of the essential importance of "culture" – learned, shared, patterned behavior transmitted from one generation to the next. All cultures are different. Westerners "know" that only the weak-kneed and yellow-bellied hide from bullies, but in other cultures it's the high-IQ and the quick-witted who pivot away from trouble.

Like the Semai, the Batek of peninsular Malaysia are high-IQ and quick-witted. "The Batek abhor interpersonal violence and have generally fled from their enemies rather than fighting back. I once asked a Batek man why their ancestors had not shot the Malay slave-raiders, who plagued them until the 1920s… His shocked answer was: 'Because it would kill them!'" (Fry, 2006: 65).

Notice this writer's state-style wording. "The Batek… have generally *fled* from their enemies rather than *fighting back*." In Western culture the word "fled" is culturally charged to suggest cowardice. Why not instead say "sidestepped," or "sashayed away from" their enemies? On the other hand, for us the words "fighting back" trigger powerful positive emotions. For most of us fighting back is the one and only proper response to enemies, Christ's "turning the other cheek" notwithstanding. My guess is, the Batek themselves would have phrased things something like this: "Rather than degrade ourselves by meeting violence with violence, we the Batek are civilized and intelligent enough to 'leave the room.'"

Not all small-scale indigenous societies are the peak of perfection. Meet the Yanomamo of Venezuela and Brazil (also known as the Yanamami, or Yanamama), until recently considered some of the world's most violent, warlike misogynists. It used to be thought the Yanomamo waged war on a regular basis and periodically blistered their wives with clubs and machetes.

Now, however, many anthropologists take exception to this earlier view of the group (see, for example, Jacque Lizot's *Tales of the Yanomami: Daily Life in the Venezuelan Forest*), which was based primarily on the 1960s fieldwork of one American anthropologist, Napoleon Chagnon (1968). Many believe now that the Yanomamo are not nearly as violent as Chagnon portrayed them. What's more, strong evidence exists that the Yanomamo are violent precisely because of their unfortunate, grotesque contacts, through the past several centuries, with large state societies (Ferguson, 2003).

Be that as it may, learning more about peaceful indigenous peoples would provide another important step toward picking our way back "home" and out of the swamp we state societies have dug ourselves into. How do the Semai, !Kung and others do it? What specific traits allow them to remain nonviolent? Equalitarian? Respectful of women, children, the elderly and the differently abled? How do their relevant beliefs, values, behaviors and attitudes compare with ours? What would it take for us to drop our starvation-culture beliefs and behaviors and take up those of the world's nonviolent people? Part of the challenge here is culture, which is like a gigantic spider web: touch one part and the whole of the woven fabric shakes and shivers. In other words, alter one part of a culture, and to a greater or lesser extent, all parts must shift and change.

Of course, if we fail to take charge of the earth's climate nothing else will matter. It's the power elite in the world's state societies who are wrecking the climate, and blocking us, their "slave" populations, from doing anything about it. "If billionaires steer climate investment to protect their wealth and private luxuries, it may be the last century we get. The alternative is to build another world on our one planet, harnessing wind, sun, and water to smash the hierarchies that oppress us and win back our future" (Aronoff et al., 2019).

Chapter 16

The Fix: Replacing Starvation Culture

After we erase starvation culture, what then? What do we drop in its place? We know we'd like to scotch social hierarchy and violence. We want equal access for all people to the necessities of life: high quality food, water, homes, and healthcare. And we're going to drive toward these goals by rearing our children in special schools – schools equipped to teach children to accept – and even demand social equality, non-violence and consensus decision making.

But then how do we organize society? What kind of social, economic and political systems would work best in a nonstate society? One thing is clear: if our work lives are undemocratic, we don't really live in democracies. In 1776 the work lives of Americans were far more democratic than they are today. As Noam Chomsky makes clear, America wasn't always a capitalist society, and the first flirtations with ideas of democracy were made by colonists who were in no way capitalists: " (T)he ideal of Jeffersonian democracy – putting aside the fact that [America] was a slave society – developed in an essentially pre-capitalist system, that is, in a society in which there was no monopolistic control, there were no significant centers of private power" (Chomsky, 1976).

Back in the eighteenth century, most Americans supported themselves by running their own small businesses. Many were farmers who owned their own land, while others were blacksmiths who owned their own blacksmith shops, chandlers who owned their own candle-making shops, and so forth. Cobblers, coopers, gunsmiths, milliners, tailors and wheelwrights didn't work as wage-slaves for corporations owned by stockholders, but freely administered their own, healthy small enterprises. They set their own work conditions. None of them were reduced to the mortifying necessity of wearing diapers to work for lack of bathroom breaks, as is the case in at least one American business concern (*Associated Press*, 2016). So at the start-line of the solution to the problem of the state, we need to train workers to run their own workplaces – their own clothing factories, offices, fruit fields and processing plants. What's more, we need to make it easier for citizens to start and run their own businesses.

Since more and more work today is done by robots, there aren't enough jobs to go around. This situation is only going to go downhill from here. The solution is a guaranteed income for everyone. As discussed in the previous chapter on erasing the state, a basic income would give all of us extra time and energy to work on dismantling the state and starvation culture. But the UBI would also help replace the state, by shifting the power balance between the power elite and the people. A universal basic income would give workers clout: with a guaranteed income, who'd play ball with an employer who refused regular bathroom breaks? How many fewer would join the military if they could find income elsewhere? "By allowing workers to walk away from a job, it could give them considerable leverage over their employers and provide them with more say in shaping the terms of their employment" (Covert, 2018). A universal basic income would provide basic life necessities only; those who wanted more than the basics would always be free to work for wages.

On top of giving everyone a free income, we also need to change the way our societies are put together. Noam Chomsky, one of the world's brightest thinkers, has a few ideas on this topic. In 2005 Chomsky was voted the world's top public intellectual – by more than 20,000 voters worldwide. This bright guy thinks we should break society down into neighborhood groups, worker groups, or maybe a combination of the two. Chomsky says his groups could work like the kibbutz, with children's homes, the same-sized paychecks for everyone, "self-management, direct worker control, integration of agriculture, industry, service, personal participation in self-management" (Chomsky, 1976).

> Beginning with the two modes of organization and control..., the workplace and... the community, one could imagine a network of workers' councils, and at a higher level, representation across the factories, or across branches of industry, or across crafts, and on to general assemblies of workers' councils that can be regional and national and international... And from another point of view, one can project a system of government that involves local assemblies – again, federated regionally, dealing with regional issues, crossing crafts, industry, trades, and so on, and again at the level of the nation or beyond. (Chomsky, 1976)

Who would lead our new councils? Most indigenous groups brook no tolerance for "great leaders," individuals worshiped as superior in all ways to others. Starvation culture seems to demand that one person, typically male, climb to and perch upon the top rung of the social-hierarchy ladder, just like the strongest male does in starving societies. It might be that such leaders are poisonous entities that help cement state societies in place. Support for this idea comes from the initially hopeful twentieth-century political revolutions in Russia, Spain and China, all of which ended miserably, with cruel dictators ruling like rabid dogs over the people.

Perhaps it's time for state societies to ditch their god-like grand leaders and replace them with councils reminiscent of those that ran the Iroquois Confederacy. Of course, a society eschewing grand pooh-bah leaders is hard for us to imagine – we've never known such societies. Equally hard to imagine: decisions being ground out not by voting (which leaves up to half the population unhappy, at best, and raging bulls at worst), but by consensus – everyone agreeing to any solution before the group accepts it as a final solution.

But children taught from birth that the group itself is grand pooh-bah, and that consensus is a superior way of reaching solutions? These children would accept such innovations like ducks take to water. If the next generation is taught from birth that everyone must get the same quality food, housing, medical care and work conditions, this is what the next generation will demand. They will work their hearts out looking for ways to live whatever ideals we teach them.

Roadblocks

To successfully pitch starvation culture out on its ear we must identify and address the major roadblocks to our end goal. Here are a few (but by no means all):

The Power Elite

Of course, one of the main roadblocks will be the power elite. Our current social systems work like well-oiled machines for them. Not only are they addicted to power, they also have the power to keep their power. Since they realize it will begin to erode the foundations of their strength, even the UBI will frighten them.

Dreams of Rags to Riches

Because they want the chance to strike it rich, ordinary people too will fight against attempts to dissolve starvation culture and the state. Thinking they have a chance of climbing to the top of the power ladder, even some of the poverty-stricken will fight to end social hierarchy. Our folklore and other media are filled with poor Cinderellas marrying the prince, poor boys trading places with rich boys, and people "pulling themselves up by their bootstraps." This needs to change. One way to begin is by realizing that the royalty in fairy tales are not royalty at all, but goddesses in disguise. Cinderella, Sleeping Beauty and Snow White are actually goddesses rescued not by a prince but by their partner in the annual sacred marriage between the pre-patriarchal goddess and her *hieros*, or mortal lover (Studebaker, 2015).

Our Love Affair with War

Even if some deny it, I suspect all of us living in state societies are subconsciously drawn to the warrior archetype. I would suggest that most of us too enjoy the release of anger and feeling of raw power that come at the start of many armed conflicts.

Protection from Other States

If we begin tearing down our state structures, how do we defend ourselves from groups lagging behind in this respect? If Europe and North America begin rearing children opposed to war and violence, how would we protect ourselves from countries still rearing children who love and demand war and violence? We need to set up mutual "disarmament" treaties vis-a-vis the state, similar to those we have with nuclear weapons.

Cultures Hate Change

Cultures change slowly, and usually only if new ideas, beliefs or norms fit in well with existing ideas, beliefs and norms. There's no getting around this, and possibly the only "solution" is to be aware of this stubborn aspect of cultural change.

Cultures Are Like Spider Webs

Touch one part of a spider web, and the whole thing shivers and shakes. Likewise, change any one part of a culture, and the whole culture changes to one degree or another. This is unnerving to people. So instead of making too many changes in your state system at once, wait until the web stops shaking a bit before moving on to further change.

No One Is to Blame

A pivotal principle of "the Fix": pointing the finger at anyone for starvation culture is senseless, unhelpful, and even harmful. We can't lay the blame at anyone's feet. First, in blaming anyone, we'd have to blame our own ancestors for "inventing" starvation culture, and ourselves for continuing to pour gas in its engines. And that would make us too depressed to roll out of bed in the morning to clean up anything, let alone something as thunderous and thorny as starvation culture.

But beyond that, it's simply the case that no one *can* be blamed. Starvation-culture people are who they are because they've been programmed into it, much like computers are programmed to behave the way they do. We humans are born without instincts, or "operating instructions." As noted in earlier chapters, birds don't have to learn how to build nests, they're born knowing all the detailed steps in the process. We, on the other hand, are born knowing zip about building shelters to stay warm, dry and safe from predators. Humans survive only by learning how, by imitating and copying the adults around them. When every single adult around you is psychotic, you learn psychotic behavior – nothing more, nothing less.

Neither can the first starvation-culture people who starved on the desert for generations be blamed. They were suffering deep psychoses, and became laser-focused on staying alive, robots programmed for nothing but survival at any cost. And this robot programing infected their children, who lacked healthy adult models, and who passed it down to their children, and so on.

As we admit no one's to blame, however, we also need to admit that all state-society citizens are responsible for the predicament we're in. The enemy is not the warmonger, elitist, or rapist. The enemy is all of us – you, me, even our loved ones. Everyone reared in a state society has learned to behave in ways that insure the continued existence of the state. We need to identify, catalog and address each one of our state-feeding behaviors – and then work hard to starve all of them out of existence.

APPENDIX 1

Starvation-Culture Timeline (dates approximate)

5900 BCE Ubaid Period begins.

4200 BCE Farming villages present all over Fertile Crescent. Population of Fertile Crescent begins to "rise rapidly." Early Uruk period begins.

4000 BCE CLIMATE CHANGE begins: Aridity begins to increase in Northern Hemisphere and subtropics.

3900 BCE 5.9 KILOYEAR EVENT ("Rapid Climate Change," or RCC). Widespread abandonment of Ubaid settlements in Khabur River region (Northern Mesopotamia).

3800 BCE Ubaid Period ends. Early Uruk ends, Middle Uruk begins (100 years after climate went berserk). By now, Urukians have replaced Ubaid people.

3500 BCE Urukians expand into Northern Mesopotamia. FIRST STATE society appears in Mesopotamia. WARFARE has begun by now (battle at Hamoukar in what is now Syria).

3200 BCE Another round of Rapid Climate Change. Population at Uruk suddenly expands tenfold.

3100 BCE End of the Uruk period. SECOND STATE society appears, in Egypt.

3000 BCE City of Uruk is now using pictographs to record economic transactions.

2900 BCE Ur Early Dynastic period begins.

2600 BCE Ur Royal Cemetery created.

2000 BCE THIRD STATE society formed, in China.

200 CE FOURTH STATE society formed, in Mexico.

APPENDIX 2

"Shafted"

Use the word "shafted" to recall the major characteristics of starvation culture:

S Strongman rules – Alpha male runs the show (as king, president, prime minister, etc.).

H Henchmen protect – Alpha rewards thugs (the power elite), who protect him.

A Adults are children – Adults depend on Daddy Alpha (are unable to mutually cooperate to solve their problems).

F Fear of starvation – People fear scarcity (so they hoard, overeat, work till they drop, etc.).

T Thugs admired – Most admired: the most efficient thief (Western movies commonly celebrate con men).

E Entertainment is pain – Entertainment consists of watching others suffer (football, hockey, dog and cock fighting).

D Dregs vs elites – Society divided into elites versus the 99%.

These seven "shafted" traits are found in the world's first city-states in Mesopotamia, in state societies today, and in the only long-starving group of humans that has been studied extensively, the Ik of Uganda. They are generally not found in healthy and relatively untouched indigenous societies like the Semai, !Kung, Inuit, Mbuti, and others.

Note about "S Strongman rules": It might seem as natural as breathing that an alpha male or female would stand at the head of any and all governments, but strongman rule is not a pan-human trait. When in the late 1780s the American colonists were adapting the Iroquois system of government for use by their own new republic, they came to the part about how the Iroquois had no one, overarching leader. Here they parted ways with the Iroquois, choosing instead to stay with the king model used by their Mother Country, England. But instead of “king,” they called their new father figure “president.”

APPENDIX 3

Glossary

5.9 Kiloyear Event – One of the worst and most rapid bouts of climate change in the history of the Holocene, the geological time period we're living in now. Occurred 5900 years ago, i.e., around 3900 BCE.

Culture – The way of life of any particular group of people. Learned, shared, and organized behavior that is passed on from one generation to the next. Unlike animals, humans are born knowing nothing, and so depend on culture to survive.

Indigenous societies – Ethnic groups that have kept their old, traditional ways that go far back into the past. The first, or earliest, inhabitants of any particular area of the world. Indigenous peoples depend on the natural resources of their area to produce their food, clothing, and other life necessities. They don't live in cities. Synonyms: traditional societies, simpler societies, hunter-gatherers, horticulturalists, primitives (pejorative), nonstates, nonstate societies.

Institutionalized warfare – A situation in which warfare has become an established custom in a society. Involves standing armies, war budgets, and a warrior class. Often the purpose of the standing army is the conquest of neighboring groups, including stealing their land and resources and enslaving their people.

Mesopotamia – The land between the Tigris and Euphrates Rivers in what is now Iraq; location of the world's first civilizations and first large cities.

Nonstates – See indigenous societies.

Simpler societies – See indigenous societies.

Starvation culture – A way of life passed down to us by certain ancestors who starved for several generations; based on the subconscious fear of never having enough (food, money; those things necessary for survival).

State, the – The result when you artificially force people into large political and territorial conglomerates. Involves the majority living packed together in large cities to work for a small power elite. The masses are controlled by this elite, either openly or surreptitiously. Instead of hunting and gathering meat and plants from the natural environment, people imprisoned in states must exchange their labor for food – primarily domesticated grains.

Traditional societies – see indigenous societies.

Ubaids – Peaceful, non-hierarchical Mesopotamians who lived immediately before the first civilizations arose, from about 5900 BCE to 3800 BCE, and who disappeared with the coming of severe, rapid climate change and starvation-culture Urukians.

Ur – One of the world's first cities, located in southern Mesopotamia near the mouth of the Euphrates River. First settled around 3800 BCE by Ubaid people but soon taken over by Urukians.

Uruk – The world's first city, located in southern Mesopotamia on the Euphrates River. First settled around 5000 BCE by Ubaids. By 3800 BCE, Urukians seemed to have gained control of Uruk completely.

Urukians – Violent, hierarchical Mesopotamians who replaced the peaceful Ubaid people around 3800 BCE. The first starvation-culture bullies.

APPENDIX 4

Questions from the Skeptics

Agriculture Did the Dirty Deed? – "Didn't the shift to war, hierarchy and other evils happen when we shifted from hunting and gathering to agriculture?" No. The people of Catalhoyuk (Catal Hoyuk, Catal Huyuk), one of the Western world's earliest agricultural settlements, appear completely innocent of war, interpersonal violence, and social hierarchy, as were the Ubaids, the early agriculturalists featured in this book. Some of the early farming societies showed a bit of social hierarchy and occasional warfare, but nothing even close to what's found in the first Mesopotamian city-states – or in state societies today. "Many agricultural village societies resisted every attempt to increase inequality. They found a way to let talented people rise to positions of prominence while still preventing the establishment of a hereditary elite" (Flannery and Marcus, 2012).

Diamond, Jared – "Jared Diamond says indigenous people are all brutal savages, and our pre-state ancestors were too. Read his *The World until Yesterday: What Can We Learn from Traditional Societies?* and you'll see!" Diamond, who has no training in anthropology, archaeology or prehistory, is hopelessly misguided. For a brutal but informed and honest assessment of his work, see prehistorian James Scott's review of *The World until Yesterday* (Scott, 2013). See also Chapter 13 in this book.

Evil is inherent – "Isn't the human species born violent and with all other evil tendencies?" Absolutely not. If we were born bad, there wouldn't be any warless, non-violent, egalitarian humans on the face of the earth. And there are. Four are described throughout this book.

Population size – "In small societies like the Semai it's easy to keep order: people want to look good in the eyes of their neighbors. It's not so easy in large countries." Monaco is less than one square mile in size and yet has murder, rape, crime, and all the other evils found in all countries (aka state societies).

Rousseau's Noble Savage – "Hasn't Rousseau's idea of the 'noble savage' been debunked?" No. Of course, not all of the simpler, indigenous societies today are free of war, violence, sexism and other evils – but many are. And those that aren't usually live close to starvation-culture people, from whom they've learned their bad behavior.

Yanamami, the – "Not all indigenous people are peaceful. The Yanamami are an indigenous tribe that's extremely violent." Your information is outdated. Many anthropologists now insist the Yanomami are not nearly as violent as originally believed. And the violence they do exhibit is the result of being used and abused by their starvation-culture neighbors. "(N)o one paying attention... still claims that Yanomami wars can be understood without taking into account the tribe's highly disrupted historical circumstances," says Rutgers University anthropologist R. Brian Ferguson (Ferguson, 2003). Prehistorian James C. Scott says Yanomami "beliefs and practices have been shaped by contact, trade goods, travel and intermarriage" with their Spanish conquerors "for much of the past three thousand years..." (Ferguson, 2003). What's more, the thesis of this book does not rest on the idea that all indigenous peoples are perfect models of humanity.

References

Abraham, Curtis. 2002. "The Mountain People Revisited." In: *New African*

Alexander, M. Wayne and William Violet. 2014. "The Marketing of People: Slave Trade in the Ancient Near East." *Journal of Business & Behavioral Sciences* 26: 2, pp. 138–155.

Alston, Philip. 2017. "Extreme Poverty in America: Read the UN Special Monitor's Report." *The Guardian* 12/15/17. <https://www.theguardian.com/world/2017/dec/15/extreme-poverty-america-un-special-monitor-report>. Accessed 1/8/18.

American Geophysical Union. "Sahara's Abrupt Desertification Started By Changes In Earth's Orbit, Accelerated By Atmospheric And Vegetation Feedbacks." *ScienceDaily* 7/12/1999. <www.sciencedaily.com/releases/1999/07/990712080500.htm>. Accessed 5/20/19.

Ang, James. 2015. "What Drives the Historical Formation and Persistent Development of Territorial States?" *The Scandinavian Journal of Economics*. 117: 4, pp. 1134–1175.

Aronoff, Kate, Alyssa Battistoni, Daniel Aldana Cohen, and Thea Riofrancos. 2019. "A Green New Deal to Win Back Our Future." *Jacobin Magazine* 2/5/19.

<https://www.jacobinmag.com/2019/02/green-new-deal-climate-change-policy>. Accessed 4/21/19.

"**Arslantepe**: An Early State Centre in Eastern Anatolia." 2015. Italian Archaeological Expedition in Eastern Anatolia. <http://www.arslantepe.com/en/vib1/>. Accessed 7/25/19.

Associated Press. 2014. "Couple To Stand Trial In 9-Year-Old Boy's Starvation Death, Weighed Less Than 17-Pounds." 10/30/14.

<https://pittsburgh.cbslocal.com/2014/10/30/couple-to-stand-trial-in-9-year-old-boys-starvation-death-weighed-less-than-17-pounds/>. Accessed 11/25/18.

Associated Press. 2014 "Hundreds attend teenage football player's funeral who died after suffering a 'big hit' during high school game." 10/8/14. <http://www.dailymail.co.uk/news/article-2783981/Hundreds-attend-NY-teen-football-players-funeral.html#ixzz3MH2KTcQ0>. Accessed 12.18.14.

Associated Press. 2016. "US Poultry Workers Wear Diapers on Job over Lack of Bathroom Breaks – Report." *The Guardian* 5/12/16. <https://www.theguardian.com/us-news/2016/may/12/poultry-workers-wear-diapers-work-bathroom-breaks>. Accessed 1/11/18.

Baadsgaard, Aubrey, Janet Monge, Samantha Cox, and Richard L. Zettler. 2011. "Human Sacrifice and Intentional Corpse Preservation in the Royal Cemetery of Ur." *Antiquity* 85: 327, pp. 27–42.

Basu, Pranab Kanti. 2007. "Political Economy of Land Grab." *Economic and Political Weekly* 42: 14.

Beachum, Lateshia. 2019. "Rats Are Capable of Driving Tiny Cars, Researchers Found. It Eases Their Anxiety." *Washington Post* 10/24/19. <https://www.washingtonpost.com/science/2019/10/24/rats-are-capable-driving-tiny-cars-researchers-found-it-eases-their-anxiety/>. Accessed 11/3/19.

Becker, Jasper. 2013. *Hungry Ghosts*. eBookPartnership.com

Belsen, Ken. 2014. "Brain Trauma to Affect One in Three Players, N.F.L. Agrees." *International New York Times* 9/12/14. <http://www.nytimes.com/2014/09/13/sports/football/actuarial-reports-in-nfl-concussion-deal-are-released.html?_r=0>. Accessed 12/18/14.

Benson, April. 2008. *To Buy or Not to Buy*. Boston & London: Trumpeter Books.

Bernbeck, Reinhard. 2009. "Class Conflict in Ancient Mesopotamia: Between Knowledge of History and Historicising Knowledge." *Anthropology of the Middle East* 4: 1, pp. 33–64.

Bordas, Camille. 2017. "They Die Young." *The New Yorker* 1/2/17.

<http://www.newyorker.com/magazine/2017/01/02/most-die-young>. Accessed 12/31/16.

Briggs, Jean L. 1995. *Never in Anger: Portrait of an Eskimo Family*. Cambridge: Harvard University Press.

Brooks, Nick. 2006. Cultural Responses to Aridity in the Middle Holocene and Increased Social Complexity. *Quaternary International* 151, pp. 29–49.

Brooks, Nick. 2010. "Human Responses to Climatically-driven Landscape Change and Resource Scarcity: Learning from the Past and Planning for the Future." In *Landscapes and Societies: Selected Cases*. I. Peter Martini and Ward Chesworth, eds. New York: Springer, pp. 43–66.

Brown, Stephen L., Glenn R. Schiraldi, and Peggy P. Wrobleski. 2009. "Association of Eating Behaviors and Obesity with Psychosocial and Familial Influences." *American Journal of Health Education* 40, pp. 80–89.

Campbell, Duncan. 2005. "Chomsky Is Voted World's Top Public Intellectual." *The Guardian* 10/18/05. <https://www.theguardian.com/world/2005/oct/18/books.highereducation>. Accessed 5/15/19.

Carneiro, Robert L. 1970. "A Theory of the Origin of the State." *Science*, New Series169: 3947, pp. 733–738. <https://canvas.brown.edu/courses/917717/files/42896431/download?wrap=1> Accessed 7/20/17.

Carter, Robert, and Philip Graham. 2010. *Beyond the Ubaid: Transformation and Integration in the Late Prehistoric Societies of the Middle East*. Chicago: University of Chicago Press.

Chagnon, Napoleon. 1968. *Yanomamo, the Fierce People*. Holt, Rinehart and Winston.

Charvat, Petr. 2002. Mesopotamia Before History. London & New York: Routledge. <https://archive.org/stream/MesopotamiaBeforeHistory/BeforeHistory_djvu.txt>. Accessed 1/8/17.

Charvat, Petr. 2008. Mesopotamia Before History. London &

New York: Routledge.

Child Maltreatment *2011*. 2012. U.S. Department of Health & Human Services Administration for Children and Families Administration on Children, Youth and Families Children's Bureau. <http://www.acf.hhs.gov/sites/default/files/cb/cm11.pdf>. Accessed 12/16/14.

Child Maltreatment *2012*. 2013. U.S. Department of Health & Human Services Administration for Children and Families Administration on Children, Youth and Families Children's Bureau. <http://www.acf.hhs.gov/sites/default/files/cb/cm2012.pdf>. Accessed 12/16/14.

Chohan, Usman W. 2017. "Universal Basic Income: A Review" *SSRN* 8/4/17. <https://ssrn.com/abstract=3013634>. Accessed 11/24/18.

Chomsky, Noam. 1976. "The Relevance of Anarcho-syndicalism." Noam Chomsky interviewed by Peter Jay. *The Jay Interview, July 25, 1976*. <https://chomsky.info/19760725/>. Accessed 11/23/18.

Chua, Amy. 2018. *Political Tribes: Group Instinct and the Fate of Nations*. New York: Penguin Press.

Cockburn, Patrick. 1997. "End of the Kibbutz Dream: Only One Camp Remains from a Total of 250." *The Independent.* <http://www.independent.co.uk/news/end-of-the-kibbutz-dream-1252506.html>. Accessed 1/12/18.

Counihan, Carole, and Penny Van Esterik, eds. 2012. *Food and Culture: A Reader*. New York: Routledge.

Covert, Bryce. 2018. "What Money Can Buy: The Promise of a Universal Basic Income—and Its Limitations." *The Nation* 8/15/18.

Dearen, Jason. 2014. "Dogfighting Thrives in Years Since Vick Case." *AP: The Big Story* 11/22/14. <http://bigstory.ap.org/article/85492d53cba147de9c81e00d061746a5/dogfighting-thrives-years-vick-case>. Accessed 12/17/14.

DeMeo, James. 1998. *Saharasia: The 4000 BCE Origins of Child*

Abuse, Sex-Repression, Warfare and Social Violence, In the Deserts of the Old World. Greensprings, Oregon: Orgone Biophysical Research Lab.

Dentan, Robert Knox. 1978. "Notes on Childhood in a Nonviolent Context." In Montagu, Ashley. *Learning Non-Aggression*. New York: Oxford University Press.

Dentan, Robert Knox. 1979. *The Semai: A Nonviolent People of Malaya*. Fieldwork Edition. New York: Holt, Rinehart and Winston. Descartes, Rene M. 2018. "Ubaid Culture in Mesopotamia." *Salem Press Encyclopedia*, 2018.

Diamond, Jared. 2012. *The World Until Yesterday: What Can We Learn from Traditional Societies?* New York: Viking.

Di Lernia, S. 2006. Building Monuments, Creating Identity: Cattle Cult as a Social Response to Rapid Environmental Changes in the Holocene Sahara. *Quaternary International* 151, pp. 50–62.

Dirks, Robert, et al. 1980. "Social Responses During Severe Food Shortages and Famine." *Current Anthropology* 21:1. <https://www.jstor.org/stable/2741740?read-now=1&seq=5#metadata_info_tab_contents>. Accessed 7/31/19.

Dirks 1994 "Hunger and Famine." *Research Frontiers in Anthropology* 4

"**Eating Disorder Statistics**." 2017. National Association of Anorexia Nervosa and Associated Disorders Webpage.
<http://www.anad.org/get-information/about-eating-disorders/eating-disorders-statistics/>. Accessed 11/12/17.

Edwards, R. Dudley and T. Desmond Williams, eds. *The Great Famine: Studies in Irish History 1845–52*. New York: New York University Press.

Emmett, Dennis, and Ashish Chandra. 2015. "Understanding Obesity Perceptions in America: An Exploratory Study of Public Perceptions of the Problem and Possible Actions for Health Product Marketers." *Hospital Topics* 93: 4, pp. 92–98.

Fagan, Brian. 2004. *The Long Summer: How Climate Changed Civilization*. New York: Basic Books.

Fagan, Brian. 2016. *Ancient Civilizations*. London: Routledge.

Fahy, Sandra. 2015. *Marching Through Suffering: Loss and Survival in North Korea*. New York: Columbia University Press.

Ferguson, R. Brian. 2003. "The Birth of War." *Natural History* 112: 6.

Ferguson, R. Brian. 2013a. "The Prehistory of War and Peace in Europe and the Near East." In Fry, Douglas, ed. 2013. *War, Peace, and Human Nature: The Convergence of Evolutionary and Cultural Views*. New York: Oxford University Press.

Ferguson, Brian. 2013b. "Pinker's List: Exaggerating Prehistoric War Mortality." In Fry, Douglas, ed. 2013. *War, Peace, and Human Nature: The Convergence of Evolutionary and Cultural Views*. New York: Oxford University Press.

Fibiger, Linda. "The Past as a Foreign Country: Bioarchaeological Perspectives on Pinker's 'Prehistoric Anarchy'." *Historical Reflections/Réflexions* Historiques 44: 1, pp. 6ff. Gale Academic Onefile, <https://link.gale.com/apps/doc/A557578629/AONE?u=maine&sid=AONE&xid=ddabcb09>. Accessed 8 Sept. 2019.

Firth, Raymond. 1959. *Social Change in Tikopia*. New York: Macmillan Co.

Firth, Raymond. 1970. *We the Tikopia*. Boston: Beacon Press.

Fitzgerald, Kathleen J. 2014. "The Continuing Significance of Race: Racial Genomics in a Postracial Era." *Humanity & Society* 38: 1, pp. 49–66.

Flannery, Kent and Joyce Marcus. 2012. *The Creation of Inequality: How Our Prehistoric Ancestors Set the Stage for Monarchy, Slavery, and Empire*. Cambridge, MA: Harvard University Press.

Flavelle, Christopher. 2019. "Climate Change Threatens the World's Food Supply, United Nations Warns." *New York Times* 8/8/19.

"**Forbes** 400: The List: 2017 Ranking." 2017. *Forbes Magazine*. <https://www.forbes.com/forbes-400/list/#version:realtime>.

Accessed 10/29/17.

Frangipane, Marcella. 2007. "Different Types of Egalitarian Societies and the Development of Inequality in Early Mesopotamia." *World Archaeology* 39: 2, pp. 151–176.

Frangipane, Marcella. 2018. "Different Trajectories in State Formation in Greater Mesopotamia: A View from Arslantepe (Turkey)." *Journal of Archaeological Research* 26: 1.

Fry, Douglas. 2006. *The Human Potential for Peace: An Anthropological Challenge to Assumptions about War and Violence*. New York: Oxford University Press.

Fry, Douglas. 2007. *Beyond War: The Human Potential for Peace*. New York: Oxford University Press.

Fry, Douglas, ed. 2013. *War, Peace, and Human Nature: The Convergence of Evolutionary and Cultural Views*. New York: Oxford University Press.

Gelderloos, Peter. 2017. *Worshiping Power: An Anarchist View of Early State Formation*. Chico, California: AK Press.

Graham, Philip J., and Alexia Smith. 2013. "A Day in the Life of an Ubaid Household: Archaeobotanical Investigations at Kenan Tepe, South-eastern Turkey." *Antiquity* 87: 336, pp. 405–417.

Griffith, Brian. 2001. *The Gardens of Their Dreams: Desertification and Culture in World History*. Halifax, Nova Scotia: Fernwood Publishing.

Grinker, Roy Richard. 2000. "In the Arms of Africa: The Life of Colin Turnbull." *Anthropology Notes, Museum of Natural History Publication for Education* 22: 1. Smithsonian Institution. <https://web.archive.org/web/20071217194239/http://artsci.wustl.edu/~anthro/courses/306/GrinkerTurnbull.html>. Accessed 7/12/19.

Haas, Jonathan, and Matthew Piscitelli. 2013. "The Prehistory of Warfare: Misled by Ethnography." In *War, Peace, and Human Nature: The Convergence of Evolutionary and Cultural Views*. Douglas P. Fry, ed. Oxford, England: Oxford University Press.

Harder, Ben. 2005. "From Famine, Schizophrenia." *Science News* 168: 6.

Hardesty, Donald L. 1997. *The Archaeology of the Donner Party*. Reno, Las Vegas, Nevada: University of Nevada Press.

Harms, William. 2007. "New Details of First Major Urban Battle Emerge Along with Clues about Civilization's Origins." Chicago: University of Chicago News Office. <http://www-news.uchicago.edu/releases/07/070116.hamoukar.shtml>. Accessed 2/9/17.

Haviland, William A., Dana Walrath, Harald E.L. Prins, and Bunny McBride. 2013. *Evolution and Prehistory: The Human Challenge*. Boston: Cengage Learning.

Hetherington, Renee and Robert G. B. Reid. 2010. *The Climate Connection: Climate Change and Modern Human Evolution*. Cambridge: Cambridge University Press.

Hoek, H. W., A. S. Brown, and E. Susser. 1998. "The Dutch Famine and Schizophrenia Spectrum Disorders." *Social Psychiatry and Psychiatric Epidemiology* 33: 8, pp. 373–79.

Holmsberg, Allan. 1969. *Nomads of the Long Bow: The Siriono of Eastern Bolivia*. Garden City, New York: The Natural History Press.

Horne, Lee. ND. "Ur and Its Treasures: The Royal Tombs." *Expedition* 40: 2. Philadelphia: University of Pennsylvania Museum of Archaeology and Anthropology. <https://www.penn.museum/sites/expedition/ur-and-its-treasures/>. Accessed 11/26/18.

Isakhan, Benjamin. 2007. "Engaging 'Primitive Democracy': Mideast Roots of Collective Governance." *Middle East Policy* 14:3, pp. 97–117.

Islam, A. 2016. "Prenatal PUFA Undernutrition and Risk of Adult Psychiatric Disorders." *Bangladesh Journal of Medical Science* 15: 3, pp. 313–19.

Issar, Arie, and Mattanyah Zohar. 2004. *Climate Change: Environment and Civilization in the Middle East*. New York:

Springer.

Jackson, Peter. 2014. "Couple Sent to Trial in Son's Starvation Death." *Associated Press* 10/30/14. <http://bigstory.ap.org/article/c2a71b588a304d209329753339e9facd/couple-sent-trial-sons-starvation-death>. Accessed 12/16/14.

Jarus, Owen. 2010. "New Discoveries Hint At 5,500 Year Old Fratricide At Hamoukar, Syria." *Archaeology News Network* 9/25/10. <https://archaeologynewsnetwork.blogspot.com/2010/09/new-discoveries-hint-at-5500-year-old.html#j8pZf7XFVH2MAoLX.99>. Accessed 2/9/17.

Jarus, Owen. 2018. "Human Sacrifices Surround Ancient Mesopotamian Tomb." *Live Science,* June 29. <https://www.livescience.com/62954-human-sacrifices-mesopotamia.html>. Accessed 7/24/19.

Jenkins, Nash. 2015. "50,000 North Koreans Work Overseas in Slave-Like Conditions, U.N. Official Says." *Time.com* 10/30/2015.

Jessri, Mahsa, Russell D. Wolfinger, Wendy Lou, and Mary R. L'Abbe. 2017. "Identification of Dietary Pattern Associated with Obesity in a Nationally Representative Survey of Canadian Adults." *American Journal of Clinical Nutrition* 105: 3, pp. 669–684.

Kennett, Douglas, and James Kennett. 2006. "Early State Formation in Southern Mesopotamia: Sea Levels, Shorelines, and Climate Change." *Journal of Island & Coastal Archaeology* 1: 1, pp. 67–99.

"Kibbutz." *Dictionary.com.* <http://www.dictionary.com/browse/kibbutz>. Accessed 1/13/18.

Kramer, Peter D. 2010. "One Man's Trash...." *New York Times Sunday Book Review* 4/23/10. <http://www.nytimes.com/2010/04/25/books/review/Kramer-t.html?ref=review&_r=0> Accessed 12/15/14.

Kress, Victoria E., Nicole Staargell, Chelsey Zoldan, and Matthew Paylo. 2016. "Hoarding Disorder: Diagnosis, Assessment, and

Treatment." *Journal of Counseling & Development* 94: 1, pp. 83–90.

Lawler, Andrew. 2016. "City of Biblical Abraham Brimmed With Trade and Riches." *National Geographic* online 3/11/16. <http://news.nationalgeographic.com/2016/03/160311-ur-iraq-trade-royal-cemetery-woolley-archaeology/> Accessed 1/9/17.

Lee, Richard B. 1984. *The Dobe !Kung*. Fort Worth: Holt, Rinehart and Winston.

Leick, Gwendolyn. 2001. *Mesopotamia: The Invention of the City*. London: Penguin Books.

Liverani, Mario. 2006. *Uruk: The First City*. London: Equinox.

Lizot, Jacques. 1991. *Tales of the Yanomami: Daily Life in the Venezuelan Forest.* Cambridge University Press.

Magee, Peter. 2014. *The Archaeology of Prehistoric Arabia: Adaptation and Social Formation from the Neolithic to the Iron Age* (Cambridge World Archaeology). Cambridge: Cambridge University Press.

Maisels, Charles Keith. 2001. *Early Civilizations of the Old World: The Formative Histories of Egypt, the Levant, Mesopotamia, India and China*. London: Routledge.

Manderson, Lenore, ed. 1986. *Shared Wealth and Symbol: Food, Culture and Society in Oceania and Southeast Asia.* Cambridge: Cambridge University Press.

Marshal, Lorna. 2000. *Nyae Nyae !Kung Beliefs and Rites.* Peabody Museum Monographs, Book 8. Cambridge, Mass.: Peabody Museum Press. <https://books.google.com/books?id=x9uAPeAmSj0C&pg=PR36&lpg=PR36&dq=Kung+storytelling&source=bl&ots=mXbpCESk0I&sig=ibHWD97eOCrHbF9j2_XYEHYjTaE&hl=en&sa=X&ei=BuGSVP38HYHdggTpvICQBA&ved=0CE0Q6AEwBw#v=onepage&q=Kung%20storytelling&f=false>. Accessed 12/18/14.

Martin, Rachel. 2017. "Will Tough New U.N. Sanctions Work Against North Korean Regime?" *Morning Edition (NPR)* 08/08/17.

Marx, Karl. 2012. *Capital*. Tampa, Florida: Aristeus Books. Translators Samuel Moore and Edward Aveling.

Max Planck Institute for the Science of Human History. "Population Dynamics and Climatic Changes in the Holocene Prehistory of Saudi Arabia." ND. <https://www.shh.mpg.de/370215/population-dynamics-and-climatic-changes-in-the-holocene-prehistory-of-saudi-arabia>. Accessed 8/3/17.

Mayer, Jane. 2016. *Dark Money: The Hidden History of the Billionaires Behind the Rise of the Radical Right*. New York: Random House.

McCullough, David. 2019. *The Pioneers: The Heroic Story of the Settlers Who Brought the American Ideal West*. New York: Simon & Schuster.

McDonagh, Marese. 2013. "Impact of Great Famine on Mental Health Examined at Science Week." *The Irish Times* 11/13/13. <https://www.irishtimes.com/news/science/impact-of-great-famine-on-mental-health-examined-at-science-week-1.1592519>. Accessed 7/25/17.

Micale, Mark S. 2018. "What Pinker Leaves Out." *Historical Reflections/Réflexions Historiques* 44:1, pp. 128ff. Gale Academic Onefile <https://link.gale.com/apps/doc/A557578639/AONE?u=maine&sid=AONE&xid=3055d923>. Accessed 8 Sept. 2019.

Mohr, Holbrook, and Garance Burke. "Faulty Reporting, Poor Oversight Let Abused Kids Suffer, Die: A Case from Maine Illustrates How Abuse Can Go On, Even When Officials Are Warned That It Is Happening." *The Associated Press*. Portland, Maine: *Portland Press Herald* 12/18/14. <http://www.pressherald.com/2014/12/17/faulty-reporting-poor-oversight-let-abused-kids-suffer-die/?utm_source=Headlines&utm_medium=email&utm_campaign=Daily>. Accessed 12/18/14.

Montagu, Ashley. 1978. *Learning Non-Aggression*. New York: Oxford University Press.

Moore, A.M.T. 2002. "Pottery Kiln Sites at al 'Ubaid and Eridu." *Iraq* 64: 69–77.

Moorey, P.R.S. 1982. *Ur 'of the Chaldees': A Revised and Updated*

Edition of Sir Leonard Woolley's Excavations at Ur. Ithaca, New York: Cornell University Press.

Moorey, P.R.S. 1984. "Where Did They Bury the Kings of the IIIrd Dynasty of Ur?" *Iraq* 46:1, pp. 1–18.

Musasizi, Simon. 2013. "Meet the Ik, Karamonja's Original Tribe on Verge of Extinction." *The Observer* [Uganda online newspaper] 10/8/13. <http://observer.ug/index.php?option=com_content&view=article&id=27912:meet-the-ik-karamojas-original-tribe-on-verge-of-extinction&catid=73:highlights&Itemid=70>. Accessed 11/28/14.

NIMH (National Institute of Mental Health). 2007. "Press Release: Violence in Schizophrenia Patients More Likely Among Those with Childhood Conduct Problems." <https://www.nimh.nih.gov/news/science-news/2007/violence-in-schizophrenia-patients-more-likely-among-those-with-childhood-conduct-problems.shtml>. Accessed 7/27/17.

Neubauer, Hendrik, ed. *The Survivors: Tribes Around the World*. Konigswinter, Germany: Tandem Verlag GmbH.

Obomsawin, Elizabeth A. 2005. "Iroquois Government and Religion." *Encyclopedia of New York State*, Peter R. Eisenstadt and Laura-Eve Moss, eds. Syracuse, NY: Syracuse University Press. *Academic OneFile*
<http://link.galegroup.com/apps/doc/A194196828/AONE?u=maine&sid=AONE&xid=e2c7880c>. Accessed 11/23/18.

Otterbein, Keith F. 2004. *How War Began*. College Station, Texas: Texas A&M University Press.

Ozbasaran, Mihriban. 2012. Book Review of *The Prehistory of Asia Minor: From Complex Hunter-Gatherers to Early Urban Societies*, by Bleda S. During. *Bulletin of the American Schools of Oriental Research* 367, pp. 87–88.

Parenti, Christian. 2012. *Tropic of Chaos: Climate Change and the New Geography of Violence*. New York: Nation Books.

"Peaceful Societies: Alternatives to Violence and War." Anthropology Department, University of Alabama at

Birmingham.
<https://cas.uab.edu/peacefulsocieties/>. Accessed 12/26/18.

Pilon, Mary, Steve Eder and Matt Krupnick. 2014. "In Death of Long Island High School Player, Perils of Football Reverberate." *International New York Times 10/2/14.*
<http://www.nytimes.com/2014/10/03/sports/long-island-high-school-player-dies-after-football-collision-officials-say.html>. Accessed 12/18/14.

Pinker, Stephen. 2012. *The Better Angels of Our Nature: Why Violence Has Declined*. New York: Penguin Books.

Piotrowski, Nancy and Leslie Tischauser. 2017. "Schizophrenia." *Magill's Medical Guide* (Online Edition), January, 2017.

Potter, Lawrence. 2010. *The Persian Gulf in History*. London: Palgrave Macmillan.

Pulkkinen, Levi. 2012. "Sons Accused after Elderly West Seattle Man Rots, Dies." Seattle, Washington: *The Seattle Post-Intelligencer (SeattlePI)* 11/16/12. <http://www.seattlepi.com/local/article/Sons-accused-after-elderly-West-Seattle-man-rots-4042130.php>. Accessed 11/25/18.

Qian, Jie, Qiang Hu, Yumei Wan, Ting Li, Mudan Wu, Zhigun Ren, and Dehua Yu. 2013. "Prevalence of Eating Disorders in the General Population: A Systematic Review." *Shanghai Archives of Psychiatry* 25: 212–223.

Reeves, Richard V. 2015. "Wealth, Inequality, and the 'Me? I'm Not Rich!' Problem". *Brookings Institute* 2/27/15. <https://www.brookings.edu/opinions/wealth-inequality-and-the-me-im-not-rich-problem/>. Accessed 10/27/17.

Reitman, Janet. 2012. "Confessions of an Ivy League Frat Boy: Inside Dartmouth's Hazing Abuses." *Rolling Stone* 3/28/12. <http://www.rollingstone.com/culture/news/confessions-of-an-ivy-league-frat-boy-inside-dartmouths-hazing-abuses-20120328>. Accessed 11/25/18.

Rice, Michael. 2011. *Archaeology of the Arabian Gulf.* Oxfordshire UK: Routledge.

Rival, Laura. 2001. "Society, Culture and Environmental Adaptability in Central and South America." *Reviews in Anthropology* 30: 4.

Roth, Randolph. "Does Better Angels of Our Nature Hold Up as History?" *Historical Reflections/Réflexions Historiques* 44:1, pp. 91ff. Gale Academic Onefile, https://link.gale.com/apps/doc/A557578636/AONE?u=maine&sid=AONE&xid=4e22cd69. Accessed 8 Sept. 2019.

Russell, Sharman Apt. 2005. *Hunger: An Unnatural History*. New York: Basic Books.

Sayce, A.H. 1930. "The Antiquity of Civilized Man." *Huxley Memorial Lecture*, pp. 269–282. Anthropological Institute of Great Britain and Ireland.

Schablitsky, Julie M. 2012. "A New Look at the Donner Party." *Archaeology* 65: 3, pp. 53–62.

Schabner, Dean. 2014. "Hazing Claiming Younger Victims." *ABCnews.go.com* 10/17/14.
<http://abcnews.go.com/US/story?id=96824>. Accessed 12/19/14.

Schutt, Bill. 2018. *Cannibalism: A Perfectly Natural History*. New York: Algonquin Books of Chapel Hill.

Schwartz, Jon. 2015. "Jimmy Carter: The US Is an Oligarchy with Unlimited Political Bribery." *The Intercept*. <https://theintercept.com/2015/07/30/jimmy-carter-u-s-oligarchy-unlimited-political-bribery/>. Accessed 1/10/18.

Schwartzstein, Peter. 2017. "Climate Change and Water Woes Drove ISIL Recruiting in Iraq." *National Geographic Newsletter* 11/14/17. <https://news.nationalgeographic.com/2017/11/climate-change-drought-drove-isis-terrorist-recruiting-iraq/>. Accessed 4.15.19.

ScienceDaily. 2014. "Genomic Diversity and Admixture Differ for Stone-age Scandinavian Foragers and Farmers." Uppsala Universitet. *ScienceDaily* 4/24/14. <www.sciencedaily.com/releases/2014/04/140424151807.htm>. Accessed 12/3/18.

ScienceDaily. 2016. "Dogs Were Domesticated Not Once,

but Twice... in Different Parts of the World." University of Oxford. *ScienceDaily* 2/6/16. <www.sciencedaily.com/releases/2016/06/160602151723.htm>. Accessed 12/3/18.

Scolforo, Mark. 2014. "Parents Charged in Death of Son Found in Home." *Associated Press* 9/30/14. <http://bigstory.ap.org/article/ad129580cbb6432b9ef7402b42817fdd/parents-charged-death-son-found-home>. Accessed 12/16/14.

Scott, James C. 2013. "Crops, Towns, Government." Review of *The World until Yesterday: What Can We Learn from Traditional Societies?* By Jared Diamond. *London Review of Books* 31: 22, 11/21/13. <https://www.lrb.co.uk/v35/n22/james-c-scott/crops-towns-government>. Accessed 4/16/19.

Scott, James C. 2017. *Against the Grain: A Deep History of the Earliest States*. New Haven and London: Yale University.

Shack, Dorothy. 2012. "Nutritional Processes and Personality Development among the Guraage of Ethiopia." In Counihan, Carole, and Penny Van Esterik, eds. 2012. *Food and Culture: A Reader*. New York: Routledge.

Shack, William. 2012. "Hunger, Anxiety, and Ritual: Deprivation and Spirit Possession among the Gurage of Ethiopia." In Counihan, Carole, and Penny Van Esterik, eds. 2012. *Food and Culture: A Reader*. New York: Routledge.

Shostak, Marjorie. 1983. *Nisa: The Life and Words of a Kung Woman*. New York: Vintage Books.

Silva, Cristina. 2017. "North Korea's Kim Jong Un Is Starving His People to Pay for Nuclear Weapons." *Newsweek* 3/23/17.

Silverstein, Yisroel. 2018. "Reign of Terror." *Salem Press Encyclopedia*.

Smail, Daniel Lord. 2018. "The Inner Demons of *The Better Angels of Our Nature*." *Historical Reflections/Réflexions Historiques* 44: 1, pp. 117ff. Gale Academic Onefile, https://link.gale.com/apps/doc/A557578638/AONE?u=maine&sid=AONE&xid=bf9175ee. Accessed 8 Sept. 2019.

Sorokin, Pitirim. 1975. *Hunger as a Factor in Human Affairs*.

Gainesville: University of Florida.

Speakman, John. 2007. " Genetics of Obesity: Five Fundamental Problems with the Famine Hypothesis." In Fantuzzi, Giamilla and Theodore Mazzone, eds. *Nutrition and Health: Adipose Tissue and Adipokines in Health and Disease.* Totowa,NJ: Humana Press Inc.

"Statistics/Data." 2014. *National Center on Elder Abuse, Administration on Aging, Health and Human Services.*
<http://www.ncea.aoa.gov/Library/Data/>. Accessed 12/18/14.

Steig, E. J. 1999. "Mid-Holocene Climate Change." *Science* 286, pp. 1485–87.

Straus, Murray, and Christine Smith. 1990. *Physical Violence in Families: Risk Factors and Adaptations to Violence in 8,145 Families*. New Brunswick, NJ: Transaction Publishers.
<http://gauss.unh.edu/~mas2/VB32.pdf>. Accessed 12/18/14.

Studebaker, Jeri. 2015. *Breaking the Mother Goose Code: How a Fairy Tale Character Fooled the World for 300 Years*. Winchester UK: John Hunt Publishing, Inc.

Susser, Ezra, David St. Clair, and Lin He. 2008. "Latent Effects of Prenatal Malnutrition on Adult Health: The Example of Schizophrenia." *Annals of the New York Academy of Sciences* 1136, pp. 185–192.

Turnbull, Colin. 1968. *The Forest People*. New York: Simon and Schuster.

Turnbull, Colin. 1972. *The Mountain People*. New York: Simon and Schuster.

Turnbull, Colin. 1976. "Turnbull Replies." *Rain* 16, pp. 4–6.

Vincent, Peter. 2009. *Saudi Arabia: An Environmental Overview.* UK: T & F Books. <http://books.google.com/books?id=Vacv2wy3yd8C&pg=PA31&lpg=PA31&dq=Saudi+Arabia+Neolithic+sites+farming&source=bl&ots=oSAjQFT7vY&sig=eCMoU3klv4whyymdPEabArNnKDA&hl=en&sa=X&ei=owB9VPwpk7-xBM61gBA&ved=0CE8Q6AEwCg#v=onepage&q=Saudi%20Arabia%20Neolithic%20sites%20farming&f=false>. Accessed

5/29/19.

Weatherford, Jack. 1988. *Indian Givers: How the Indians of the Americas Transformed the World.* New York: Fawcett Columbine.

Mental Health Weekly Digest. 2018. "Reports Summarize Transcultural Psychiatry Study Results from Karolinska Institute (A Transcultural Study of Hoarding Disorder: Insights from the United Kingdom, Spain, Japan, and Brazil)." 5/7/18 p. 317. *Gale OneFile: Health and Medicine*. <https://link.gale.com/apps/doc/A537525140/HRCA?u=maine&sid=HRCA&xid=13a213bc>. Accessed 10/21/19.

Werrell, Caitlin E., and Francesco Femia. 2019. "Climate Change Raises Conflict Concerns. *The UNESCO Courier*.
<https://en.unesco.org/courier/2018-2/climate-change-raises-conflict-concerns>. Accessed 4/15/19.

Wesler, Kit. W. 2012. *An Archaeology of Religion*. Lanham, MD: University Press of America. <https://books.google.com/books?id=5XGTDAAAQBAJ&printsec=frontcover&dq=An+Archaeology+of+Religion&hl=en&sa=X&ved=0ahUKEwj69K6z38HiAhUPS6wKHWM9DhUQ6AEILzAB#v=onepage&q=An%2-0Archaeology%20of%20Religion&f=false>. Accessed 5/29/19.

Whoriskey, Peter. 2017. "North Korea's 'Humanitarian' Exports Paid for Weapons Programs, U.S. Says." *Washington Post* 8/6/17. <https://www.washingtonpost.com/business/economy/north-koreas-humanitarian-exports-paid-for-weapons-programs-us-says/2017/08/05/deeb7f3e-761d-11e7-9eac-d56bd5568db8_story.html?utm_term=.87cf431fa0c8>. Accessed 8/7/17.

Wilford, John Noble. 2007. "Ruins in Northern Syria Bear the Scars of a City's Final Battle." *New York Times* 1/16/07.
<http://www-news.uchicago.edu/citations/07/070116.hamoukar-nyt.html>. Accessed 2/9/17.

Wilford, John Noble. 2009. "At Ur, Ritual Deaths That Were Anything but Serene." *The New York Times* 10/26/90. <http://

www.nytimes.com/2009/10/27/science/27ur.html>. Accessed 1/8/17.

Wilkinson, T. 1999. *Early Dynastic Egypt*. London: Routledge.

Wilstein, Matt. 2018. "Welcome to 'Corporate': Inside the Darkest Workplace Comedy Ever." *The Daily Beast* 1/13/18. https://www.thedailybeast.com/welcome-to-corporate-inside-the-darkest-workplace-comedy-ever?ref=home>. Accessed 1/14/18.

Winerip, Michael. 2012. "When a Hazing Goes Very Wrong." *New York Times* 4/12/12. <http://www.nytimes.com/2012/04/15/education/edlife/a-hazing-at-cornell.html?pagewanted=all&_r=0>. Accessed 12/20/14.

Wood, Graeme. 2011. "The Fortunate Ones: Does Great Wealth Bring Fulfillment?" *The Atlantic* 307: 3, pp. 72–78.

Woolley, Leonard. 1934. *Ur Excavations Vol. II: The Royal Cemetery*. Trustees of the British Museum and the Museum of the University of Pennsylvania.

Woolley, Leonard. 1965. *Excavations at Ur: A Record of Twelve Years' Work*. New York: Thomas Y. Crowell Company.

Young, Michael W. 1986. "'The Worst Disease': The Cultural Definition of Hunger in Kalauna." In Manderson, Lenore, ed. 1986. *Shared Wealth and Symbol: Food, Culture and Society in Oceania and Southeast Asia*. Cambridge: Cambridge University Press.

Zinkina, Julia, Andrey Korotayev and Alexey Andreev. 2016. "Circumscription Theory of the Origins of the State: A Cross-Cultural Re-Analysis." *Cliodynamics* 7: 2, pp. 187–203. Oakland, California: University of California Press.

Zorich, Zach. 2006. "Relics of the Very First War." *Discover* 27: 3, p. 12.

Sources on the Ik, Inuit, Semai, !Kung and Mbuti

Abraham, Curtis. 2002. "The Mountain People Revisited." In: *New African* February, 2002.

Briggs, Jean L. 1995. *Never in Anger: Portrait of an Eskimo Family*. Cambridge: Harvard University Press.

Dentan, Robert Knox. 1978. "Notes on Childhood in a Nonviolent Context." In Montagu, Ashley. *Learning Non-Aggression*. New York: Oxford University Press.

Dentan, Robert Knox. 1979. *The Semai: A Nonviolent People of Malaya*. Fieldwork Edition. New York: Holt, Rinehart and Winston.

Fry, Douglas. 2006. *The Human Potential for Peace: An Anthropological Challenge to Assumptions about War and Violence*. New York: Oxford University Press. [Semai]

Heine, Bernd. 1985. "The Mountain People: Some Notes on the Ik of North-Eastern Uganda." *Africa* 55: 1.

Lee, Richard B. 1984. *The Dobe Kung*. Fort Worth: Holt, Rinehart And Winston.

Montagu, Ashley. 1978. *Learning Non-Aggression: The Experience of Non-Literate Societies*. New York: Oxford University Press. [!Kung, Mbuti, Semai, Inuit]

Robarchek, Clayton A. 2013. "A Community of Interests: Semai Conflict Resolution." In Douglas Fry and Kaj Bjorkqvist, eds., *Cultural Variation in Conflict Resolution: Alternatives to Violence*. Psychology Press.

Turnbull, Colin. 1968. *The Forest People*. New York: Simon and Schuster. [Mbuti]

Turnbull, Colin. 1972. *The Mountain People*. New York: Simon and Schuster. [Ik]

Turnbull, Colin. 1976. "Turnbull Replies." *Rain* 16, pp. 4–6. [Ik]

Willerslev, Rane, and Lotte Meinert. 2017. "Understanding

Hunger with Ik Elders and Turnbull's *The Mountain People*." *Ethnos: Journal of Anthropology* 82: 5.

ACADEMIC AND SPECIALIST

Iff Books publishes non-fiction. It aims to work with authors and titles that augment our understanding of the human condition, society and civilisation, and the world or universe in which we live.
If you have enjoyed this book, why not tell other readers by posting a review on your preferred book site.
Recent bestsellers from Iff Books are:

Why Materialism Is Baloney
How true skeptics know there is no death and fathom answers to life, the universe, and everything
Bernardo Kastrup
A hard-nosed, logical, and skeptic non-materialist metaphysics, according to which the body is in mind, not mind in the body.
Paperback: 978-1-78279-362-5 ebook: 978-1-78279-361-8

The Fall
Steve Taylor
The Fall discusses human achievement versus the issues of war, patriarchy and social inequality.
Paperback: 978-1-78535-804-3 ebook: 978-1-78535-805-0

Brief Peeks Beyond
Critical essays on metaphysics, neuroscience, free will, skepticism and culture
Bernardo Kastrup
An incisive, original, compelling alternative to current mainstream cultural views and assumptions.
Paperback: 978-1-78535-018-4 ebook: 978-1-78535-019-1

Framespotting

Changing how you look at things changes how you see them

Laurence & Alison Matthews

A punchy, upbeat guide to framespotting. Spot deceptions and hidden assumptions; swap growth for growing up. See and be free.

Paperback: 978-1-78279-689-3 ebook: 978-1-78279-822-4

Is There an Afterlife?

David Fontana

Is there an Afterlife? If so what is it like? How do Western ideas of the afterlife compare with Eastern? David Fontana presents the historical and contemporary evidence for survival of physical death.

Paperback: 978-1-90381-690-5

Nothing Matters

a book about nothing

Ronald Green

Thinking about Nothing opens the world to everything by illuminating new angles to old problems and stimulating new ways of thinking.

Paperback: 978-1-84694-707-0 ebook: 978-1-78099-016-3

Panpsychism

The Philosophy of the Sensuous Cosmos

Peter Ells

Are free will and mind chimeras? This book, anti-materialistic but respecting science, answers: No! Mind is foundational to all existence.

Paperback: 978-1-84694-505-2 ebook: 978-1-78099-018-7

Punk Science

Inside the Mind of God

Manjir Samanta-Laughton

Many have experienced unexplainable phenomena; God, psychic abilities, extraordinary healing and angelic encounters. Can cutting-edge science actually explain phenomena previously thought of as 'paranormal'?

Paperback: 978-1-90504-793-2

The Vagabond Spirit of Poetry

Edward Clarke

Spend time with the wisest poets of the modern age and of the past, and let Edward Clarke remind you of the importance of poetry in our industrialized world.

Paperback: 978-1-78279-370-0 ebook: 978-1-78279-369-4

Readers of ebooks can buy or view any of these bestsellers by clicking on the live link in the title. Most titles are published in paperback and as an ebook. Paperbacks are available in traditional bookshops. Both print and ebook formats are available online.

Find more titles and sign up to our readers' newsletter at http://www.johnhuntpublishing.com/non-fiction

Follow us on Facebook at https://www.facebook.com/JHPNonFiction

and Twitter at https://twitter.com/JHPNonFiction